Livin' My Dream

Livin' My Dream

Stories That Illustrate What I Believe

DAVID P. BENZ

British Library Cataloguing in Publication Information available

Library of Congress Cataloging-in-Publication Data available

ISBN 978-0-5787-8135-8 (paperback)
ISBN 978-0-5787-8136-5 (e-book)

∞™ The paper used in this publication meets the minimum requirements of American National Standard for Information Sciences—Permanence of Paper for Printed Library Materials, ANSI/NISO Z39.48-1992

Printed in the United States of America

Dedication

For Jess and Rob – This is what your Dad believes and the stories that have shaped who I am. I believe I have passed along most of these stories and all of these lessons previously. I hope that you will pass them along to those important in your lives.

To Joyce – Thank you. We have chosen wisely. All my love, forever.

I wanted my kids to have what I didn't as a kid – I wonder what Jess and Rob want for their children?

Thank You

Special thanks to Marilyn Burkley who edited the manuscript and Jen Huppert who created the covers and formatted the interior. Grateful for your guidance and patience during this process.

Contents

David at 2

Introduction

How ya doing, Benzy? Livin' the dream, Homie.

I think most people who say they are living the dream mean it in a sarcastic way. They don't really mean it. But I really do feel like I'm living the dream, my dream, the life I've made. I dreamt as a kid about marrying my sweetheart, having two children, being successful in a career, and living happily ever after, just like in the movies and fairy tales. But there was one thing missing in my life. You see, I wanted what I did not have at home. What I had was an ever-changing parade of adult men in my life, and what I always wanted was a dad.

So, this book is meant to be two things: first, a chronicle of my life for my children and grandchildren, to tell my story, if you will. Second, it's a retelling of stories from my life to help reinforce or explain why I believe what I do. Life unfolds in ways we never imagined, beyond our wildest dreams sometimes. Being grounded in what matters and what's important to us helps to navigate the daily grind of everyday life. Not every day is full of sunshine; it takes the rainy days to really appreciate the sunny ones.

I'm "livin' my dream" every day.

I like stories, and everyone has their own. I am especially fond of stories that carry meaning. When what you believe is rooted in your own personal stories, it is very easy for your beliefs to become the backbone of your being, that which everything else sits and rests on.

Everyone has a story, and individual stories make up their lives. Over time, some stories become history. The Bible is full of meaningful stories. Ancient Greek and Roman mythology are stories passed from one generation to the next. Somewhere down the line they were written down. The stories that survive typically are filled with meaning or lessons to be learned, like Aesop's fables. Stories are remembered and become memories, memories that you hold dear to your heart because of their meaning and how your story interacts with them.

These are the stories that have shaped who I've become and what I believe. This is my story.

Early On

"John Howland was born about 1599, probably in Fenstanton, Huntingdon [England]. He came on the *Mayflower* in 1620 as a manservant of Governor John Carver. During the *Mayflower*'s voyage, Howland fell overboard during a storm, and was almost lost at sea—but . . . he managed to grab hold of the topsail halyards, giving the crew enough time to rescue him with a boat-hook." This is the opening paragraph from the John Howland web page on Mayflowerhistory.com. Howland is written about in middle and high school history books, and certainly most of us have heard about the *Mayflower.*

I am a descendant of this man by way of my mother and grandmother. My niece Brittany had a family tree lesson in high school, and during her extensive research she discovered this lineage. (I am not sure Gram knew any family history much further back than *her* grandmother, this information about John Howland having never been told to my mother or me. How could we not have known this? That seems odd to me.) Anyway, along our line of ancestors is John Howland, darn near lost from the Mayflower, signer of the Mayflower Compact, and buried at Plymouth Rock. Other descendants of Howland include Nathaniel Gorham, who was an influential member of the Continental Congress and a signee of the U.S. Constitution; Ephraim Gorham, who fought in the Revolutionary War; Shubael Gorham, who fought in the War of 1812; and Warren Gorham, a soldier in Company 1 of the 7th Michigan Cavalry in the Civil War. I'm in the thirteenth generation of John Howland's descendants in America, along with all my cousins on Gram's side. In fact, my cousin Carl reminds me of John Howland. They both have survived near-death experiences.

It is hard to put into words what having this knowledge means. It makes me feel proud of my family's contributions to the history of this country. It also means nothing in the day-to-day realities of everyday life. If nothing else, it can be interesting to know your ancestry.

I was born David Paul Shoemaker on February 5, 1960, at Sparrow Hospital in East Lansing, Michigan. My dad was Paul Shoemaker; he was attending Michigan State University, working toward an engineering degree. He and Mom, Beth Lorraine Rose, had married two weeks after she graduated from Waterford High School in 1957. They had met while double-dating with Mom's older sister Gloria. Paul grew up in White Lake, Michigan. He graduated from Milford High in 1954 as class president while lettering in basketball.

Waterford High School Sophomore Is Named State Cherry Pie Champion

A 15-year-old Waterford Township girl who got an early start in the state's 23rd annual Cherry Pie Baking Contest yesterday walked off with top honors today.

Beth Lorraine Rose, a high school sophomore, entered the contest at Grand Rapids yesterday when she clanged the oven door shut on her entry, first in the competition.

She was named winner over 81 other contestants today, baking her way into representing Michigan in the national contest slated for next Friday in Chicago.

Along with the honors goes a $150 scholarship, which George S. McIntyre, director of the Michigan State Department of Agriculture presented to her.

The daughter of Mr. and Mrs. Leon Rose of North Cass Lake Road, Beth is a member of the Waterford 4-H Club.

Contest officials wouldn't reveal how many points she received out of the 1,000 maximum, "but you can bet she received more than 950," contest chairman Reed M. Roberts said.

Each contestant was judged on three main points — method of preparation of their pie, quality of the pie, and personal qualifications. The pie itself accounted for about two-thirds of the maximum number of points scored, while the other two classifications accounted for the remaining points.

Runners-up were Darlene Hansen, 17, of Manistee County, second, and Carol Dickman, 16, of Kent County, in third place.

Late yesterday Beth, a blue-eyed brunette, was announced as one of the eight finalists in the contest, before parlaying her recipe and oven temperature to the pay-off in the contest sponsored by the Michigan Canners and Freezers Assn. and the Michigan Cherry Commission.

The bake-off was the climax of scores of city and county cherry pie baking contests all over the state in which an estimated 4,000 girls and at least one boy participated.

Richard Wood, a Mt. Pleasant high school athlete, was co-winner of the Isabella County contest but couldn't come to the state contest because it was only open to girls.

Pontiac Press Photo

BETH ROSE
Michigan Cherry Pie Champion

Pontiac Press – Cherry Pie Queen – 1954

Mom was born in 1939 and grew up in the house her dad had built on Cass Lake Road in Waterford, Michigan. She was the fifth of six children: Leon, Carl, Marshall, Gloria, Mom, and Larry. Mom was active in 4H and loved baking at home. She learned all her cooking skills from Gram. Mom won the Michigan Cherry Pie Queen title when she was fifteen. She told me that at the National Cherry Pie Contest, the hot TV lights in the studio raised the temperature of her butter, and her crust suffered, as did that of many other contestants. Gram was upset that she had not thought of that and warned Mom ahead of time.

Mom lettered in field hockey and was the editor of the school yearbook, which won a National Medal of

Mom and Paul – Wedding Day – 1957

Distinction. Mom told me that she loved playing with dolls and that she got her last one on Christmas when she was thirteen.

Paul, my dad, was the middle child of Mary and Paul Shoemaker. His sister Joan was three years older and his sister Bonnie was eight years younger. I'm just now realizing I don't know much about Paul's life growing up, or about his parents and their upbringing. After Paul graduated from MSU, we moved to San Diego, California, and he began his engineering career at General Dynamics.

My sister, Jenifer Beth, was born on March 24, 1962. We moved to the Cary, North Carolina, area shortly after Jen was born. I don't recall much other than thunderstorms. It would thunder for hours. I think I can recall the JFK funeral procession that was televised. Little John's salute as his dad passed by made an impression. But I've seen that footage and those photos many times over the years; perhaps my timing is off.

Not all was happily ever after with Mom and Paul. In 1965, Mom, Jen, and I moved back to Michigan and lived with Mom's oldest brother, Leon, and his family in Farmington. Uncle Leon, Aunt Margaret, Sandy, Cindy, Randy, Candy, and Lindy, plus the three of us, made ten. What a houseful that was! All of us kids would sit around the black-and-white television after school and watch *Mickey Mouse.*

Mom and Paul were officially divorced on January 1, 1966. After the divorce, Mom had to figure out how to be a single working mother without a college degree. The first place the three of us lived together on our own was a townhouse in Pontiac, right across the side street from St. Joseph Hospital. This was 1967, and the riots in Detroit were making Mom's mother and father nervous, so we moved in with Gram and Gramps for the summer of '67.

Gram and Gramps

Gram and Gramps would be major influences on who I became. Early on I knew, or somehow learned, that there were other people in the world who would provide guidance and influence in addition to Mom. It was clear to me quite early that Gram and Gramps had a very successful marriage. What did this kid know about marriage? I could see a glint in Gramp's eyes when he talked about Gram's baking. Gram would stand behind the chair Gramps was sitting in to pick at his blackheads while he watched the console TV. They would banter back and forth with each other while playing euchre with their neighbor friends.

Gram was born Zelna Mae Van Blarcom on July 1, 1907, and married Leon R. Rose on December 17, 1923. Gram was sixteen when she married Gramps, who was fifteen. Imagine all the history they knew as part of their life. From horse-drawn carriages to cars, from no such thing as airplanes to commercial aviation, radio, TV. Trying to make ends meet with a young family during the Depression. Gramps worked three jobs, I've been told. They lived from the beginning of the Industrial Revolution to the dawn of the Digital Age.

Gram and Gramps were always a part of my life growing up. They measured how I was growing by marking my progress up the kitchen cabinet, until my chin was over the top of the counter. There were sleepovers with homemade milkshakes before bed, and game-playing. Oh, did we play games—Jen and I, with or without Gram and Gramps. Card games, board games. Gramps made up a game of his

Rose Family – circa early 1940's – top row Uncle Carl, Gramps, Uncle Leon, middle row Uncle Marshall, Gram, front row: Mom (Bethie), Uncle Larry, Aunt Gloria

own that he called "Dirty Board." It was similar to Sorry, using marbles, dice, and moving around the board. He made the board himself out in his shop in the garage.

The house Mom grew up in was built by Gramps. He was a product of the Great Depression. Somehow he raised six kids, working for Fisher Body, doing side jobs in his garage. He was a Navy welder and was certified in using difficult metals to weld. He could and did make just about anything. Their cabin on Lily Lake near Harrison is another example of his craftsmanship. It had the best fireplace ever. Even Paul helped Gramps with it; it seems everyone in the family helped in some fashion. Mom can remember digging part of the foundation with a shovel.

I can still hear Gramps today: "God dammit, David, I just untangled that fishing line, I don't understand how you can . . ." all while his daily cigar was stuck in his mouth and he was working on or fixing something. It seems I was good at tangling the line, not casting.

It was at the cabin that I learned how to play euchre, a card game seemingly known only to Michiganders. My love for perch stems from Lily Lake—fishing for them, Gram pan frying 'em for dinner. Jen and I often spent weekends with Gram and Gramps up at the lake. We would spend Friday night at their house. Gram would wake us up when it was still dark, dump us in the car still in our jammies, and away we'd go. By the time we woke up, we were there.

One Saturday, Jen and I were out playing in the yard, Gram was in the kitchen cooking, and Gramps was in the shed fixing or making something. Out of the clear blue sky, Jen screamed at the top of her lungs, that "a bear is going to get me" scream. She had seen a snake in the water right near the edge of the little beach area. I came running around the corner just in time. Gramps had grabbed the old .410 single-shot shotgun. I saw him load it while walking briskly toward the snake. He took aim, and bang, just like that, no more snake. Jen ran inside, Gramps used his fishing net to haul away what was left of the snake, and it only took me a minute to get back to what I was doing. Looking back, Lily Lake memories are the reason why I have a cottage on a lake today.

I tell you all about Gram and Gramps because my first major goal in life was to have one marriage. I could see that Mom wasn't the example. But heck, by the time I was ten, Gram and Gramps had been married for over fifty years, so it was sure possible, and to me it seemed a better way to go.

During the time when we lived in the townhouse, Mom married Dallas

Paul teaching David how to use a saw. The Lily Lake cabin in the background. 1963

Merrick. They married on May 1, 1967, and that winter Mom was pregnant. Their marriage didn't last long. They were divorced on May 1, 1968. When she came home from the hospital, Mom and Dallas told Jen and me that she had miscarried. Later we would learn that she gave her newborn baby girl up for adoption. Later in life Nancy contacted Mom and saw her and Dallas a few times. Jen decided she wanted to meet her as well. I chose not to meet her. She ultimately went back to her family but was grateful for the opportunity to have met her biological mother and father.

Dallas had come and gone, and Mom said she was working on a new plan.

Off to School

We moved to an apartment in Auburn Heights on South Boulevard near Opdyke Road, and I started first grade at Avondale Elementary School. Mom started working for the Oakland County School System as a secretary. During this time, Jen and I would go to the home of a local couple, Barb and Bob, who were friends of Uncle Leon's, and they would provide after-school day care. Our apartment was at the edge of the subdivision where Barb and Bob lived, and they would keep us entertained and fed until Mom picked us up after her workday was finished. I would play catch with Bob in their tiny backyard. Both Jen and I developed friends in the neighborhood and would play with them on the weekends, since our apartment was so close.

One of Barb's rules was that you had to clean your plate. I never got to put the food on my plate in the first place and didn't think that rule was fair. I didn't get it then and I don't now. I was being stubborn one day and decided that I was not going to eat the vegetables. Barb said, "Fine, you sit right there. Jen, you can be excused. David, you can either finish your plate and move along or sit right there and wait till your mother picks you up." I waited.

When I was in first and second grade at the old Avondale Elementary near Squirrel and Auburn, there was a flower lady. She lived in a small house with an attached greenhouse near the school and sold cacti and plants from her house. When school was out for the day, the kids would go into her house and buy things for their homes and for special occasions. I can't imagine that kind of thing now.

A new elementary school was built right in the center of the neighborhood, in time for the start of third grade. That was my first year in Cub Scouts. I liked it—earning badges was rewarding, learning skills. We stayed in the apartment for two years. This was starting to feel like home.

I have very vivid memories of the 1968 World Series: Tigers vs. Cardinals. Our teacher allowed us to listen to the games in school on the radio. Yes, they played day games back then. The whole class was on edge listening to Ernie Harwell's broadcast. Paul somehow got tickets to game 5. This was Monday, October 7, 1968. I don't remember any buildup or anticipation of waiting to go to the game. I don't remember Paul picking me up, or the ride to Tiger Stadium. I only remember just Dad and I being at the game. This is my very best memory of Paul to this day. I felt like a typical kid getting to do something really cool with his dad, just like other kids I knew.

We got to the stadium early. At this point I was a huge baseball fan. I was eight years old, had my Tiger D hat on, and of course I brought my glove in case I could catch a ball. I had just finished my first season of T-ball. I knew all the players from both sides, had some of their baseball cards. Al Kaline was my favorite Tiger. Lou Brock was my favorite Cardinal. We sat in the lower deck at old Tiger Stadium in left field, just under the upper deck about eight rows up. We were sitting right next to one of the walkways leading down to the concourse area. We grabbed a program, got some food from the concourse, and found our seats for the Tigers' batting practice. How cool was this—out of school for a Monday World Series day game. Watching the stands fill up, the electricity in the stadium, the players going through their pregame routines, watching for home runs during batting practice. *Maybe one will come my way. I'll be ready to catch it.*

One came close. I don't remember who hit it. I watch it off the bat, coming this way. *Definitely coming this way.* I stand up. I'm right up against the rail, leaning over, and the ball goes right down the concourse on the fly. I was so close. Only a foot or two away.

I recall answering the questions of a man standing next to me on the walkway side of the railing. It was a local newspaper writer, out interviewing the fans. He started by asking me, "Who's your favorite Tiger?"

"Al Kaline."

"Who's your favorite Cardinal?"

"Lou Brock." He's taking notes.

"Can the Tigers win, being down three games to one?"

"Yes." And so on for a few more questions before he was off to the next fan. The Tigers went on to win that game, thanks to left fielder Willie Horton's throw to catcher Bill Freehan, who collided with Lou Brock at home plate. Out! We win game 5.

I looked in the newspaper the next couple of days to see if I was mentioned in the article. No such luck. We won games 6 and 7 to win the World Series. That was the year Denny McLain went 31–6 and won the American League Cy Young Award. And Mickey Lolich won three World Series games and the World Series MVP. The Tigers had taken down the previous year's champs and National League Cy Young winner Bob Gibson. That World Series is also notable in that manager Mayo Smith moved good-hitting center-fielder Mickey Stanley to shortstop to replace light-hitting Ray Oyler. That kind of move would not be made in today's World Series. All was right with the world; my team had just won the World Series, and I got to hang out with my dad for the day.

I have thought about this day many times in my life. I don't remember being picked up, or the drive to the stadium. I remember being at the stadium and the game, the interview, the batting practice ball being so close. The fly ball to Horton, the throw to Freehan—I couldn't see the crash at home plate over the taller adults in front of me. I remember leaving the stadium as happy as an eight-year-old boy can be. I don't remember the drive home. It's odd what we remember and what we don't.

Jen and I would visit Paul and his new wife in their house in Grosse Pointe during this time in our lives. They had a house just off Vernier Road near Charlevoix Avenue. We visited a half dozen or so times. It might have been more, but I don't have a good recollection. There was a school nearby where we played ball, throwing a ball against a wall of the school. I loved playing baseball. I visited that house enough times so that later in life I would drive by that neighborhood and could damn near remember the exact house. Paul had a new wife but no other children at this point and was working for Uniroyal Tire in Detroit.

By the end of 1968, Mom was seeing another man. She had been doing her best raising Jen and me. We had a routine and things seemed to be ok. To pick up some extra bucks, Mom started hostessing for Uncle Marshall at his restaurant in downtown Birmingham, the Beef N Bun. This was a dimly lit burger joint, and a good one if I remember right. Fresh burgers. Homemade potato chips, served hot. Gramps had made Marshall a wooden burger form for a one-third-pound patty, so they all were the same size and shape. I still have the one he made for me.

During one of Mom's hostess shifts, a very tall man asked to be seated where it would be light enough to read while eating lunch. The restaurant was dark, not a good place to read at all. Mom told him the best place to read would be to go to the library, but "I can seat you in the best spot we have available." Seems Mom made an impression. He would return, this time to ask if she was available to come to work for his company, Design Origins Inc. (D.O.). Just like that, Mom had a new job. Mom met Doug Benz while they both worked at D.O. for Hardy Brodersen, the man from the restaurant. I would later work for and mentor under Hardy.

Mom and Doug fell in love and got married on December 31, 1968. I would forever be linked to Doug, Hardy, and Design Origins—I just didn't know it yet. I've always liked this story. I've heard it told a number of times, from both Mom's and Hardy's perspectives. I liked that Mom told Hardy this wasn't the place to read. I like that Hardy respected her answer, and that a lifelong connection was made. An early example of a story with meaning.

Name Change

My name would change in the summer of 1969. Mom had married Doug Benz. I'm not sure about the timing of the meeting and dating part, but sometime in July or August, Mom and Doug sat down with Jen and me and talked about what they wanted to happen. They had gotten married, and we would be adopted by Doug if we were willing. We were going to move into this cool old house in Birmingham and start fresh as a new family. Sounded good to both of us. It seemed like we were seeing Paul less frequently. Being part of a "typical" family sounded good to me. Jen and I were both all in, as I recall it now.

The official adoption and ceremony were a bit surreal. The judge explained everything to Jen and me to make sure we understood and agreed. Then she announced it was official and we were now David and Jenifer Benz. When the new birth certificates arrived, I was surprised that Paul's name was nowhere on the document, as if he were never involved. There were no "birth father" or "adoptive father" designations; it was as if Doug had always been my father. That seemed weird to me then, and I still don't like it today.

We moved into the old house in Birmingham, we had new last names, we were part of a new family, a new school, with a new beginning. I started fourth grade at Baldwin Elementary School, Jen second grade. We walked together to school for the first few weeks. We made new friends—there were kids everywhere. In this district there were about nine elementary schools, five junior highs, and

David's 4th grade class at Baldwin Elementary. 1969

two high schools. I can't believe how many kids there were, more than I had ever seen. Kids of all ages, riding their bikes. Jen and I settled in—this was what I thought family looked like.

Except for one thing. Doug asked Jen and me to call him either Dad or Mr. Benz. Those were the only two choices we had. We settled on Dad. But I didn't like being told the words I had to use. It felt forced. I didn't understand why it was so important. At first, I avoided using either word. But after a few months, calling Doug "Dad" happened all on its own. Everything else about this new arrangement I was comfortable with.

The house was old and had a few very odd features. The small damp basement with an ancient furnace was not a fun place to do laundry but was typical of the area at the time. A door on the first floor opened to the basement, but there were no stairs or any other way down. So why was there a door? Another odd item was the second-floor outdoor patio space. There were no safety railings to prevent a fall. Doug had a couple of carpenters from D.O. work on the house for two summers. By the end of the second summer the house had been reworked from top to bottom and Jen and I had become friends with Harry and Tony, the two carpenters. In the summer, Mom and Dad went to work, and we stayed home and played with our neighborhood friends.

Fitting In

By fifth grade I had joined the safety program and helped the younger kids cross the street to get to and from school. On cold mornings, the safeties got to have hot chocolate in the cafeteria before going to class late, with permission. I ran for Safety Captain in sixth grade. I lost to a classmate who went on to become part of the U.S. Secret Service. Looking back, it seems like the right guy won! But being a lieutenant had its advantages. I got to leave early at the end of class to get the safeties organized and in their positions before school let out.

I would meet two very important people in my life at Baldwin, and they remain close friends to this day: Drew and Kathy. We are part of a larger group of high school friends that continue to get together.

I had my first crush on a girl, Joanne, in sixth grade. We played spin the bottle at her house and had a first kiss. Her family moved to Minnesota the following year.

The gym at Baldwin Elementary was the best ever. When the building was built, it was the first Birmingham High School. There was a big formal front entrance and foyer; the building was three stories high with huge windows around the whole perimeter. Kindergarten and first grade were on the first floor, second, third, and fourth grade on the second floor, fifth and sixth grade on the third floor. The gym was a combination gym/auditorium with a big stage for assemblies and plays. We had basketball hoops at eight, nine, and ten feet. The best part was the wooden track above the floor. It circled the whole gym with banked corners;

you could look over the railing and see who was in the gym. We would have relay races on the track—it was so much fun. I can't see anything like that being allowed in an elementary school now.

Baldwin was closed at the end of the year due to decreasing enrollment in the district. We were the last sixth graders to graduate from Baldwin—the end of the baby boomers.

The Birmingham Fair has been held in May in Shain Park in downtown Birmingham since . . . well, forever, and still is today. Baldwin Elementary was a block and a half away from the park. From the third floor school rooms, you could see the park. For the two or three days while the fair was being set up, it was very difficult to pay attention in class, what with trying to watch all the activity and see what rides were going where. During this time, going to the park during school hours was prohibited and subject to suspension. One kid just had to go. He was bound and determined. He got caught and, yes, was suspended. No one did that again.

While in elementary school I started taking things apart and putting them back together. Trying to make all the pieces fit and hoping not to have any parts left over. Or making models of cars, boats, and planes and even painting them as I got older. Sometimes they were store-bought, and sometimes I just made things up. A neighbor friend and I would make things in his basement—time travel machines, robots. We put lights and timers on them and painted them up. Everything was held together with duct tape and glue.

Bicycles were the mode of transportation in my childhood. We would ride everywhere. I rode my bike to baseball games. The first book I ever read was a description of how to play each position on the field. I could play anywhere. At this stage of my life, at ten to twelve years old, I wanted to be a professional baseball player. Al Kaline was my idol. Baseball was very important to me. I could escape into a world where there were no troubles. In game uniform, mitt on the handlebars, I would ride up Lincoln, across Woodward, across Adams, across Eaton, to the park where we played our Little League games, behind the skating rink. Mom would come to the games often, but Dad never seemed to be able to make it. That has always bugged me. I was a happy kid from very early on; my friends would say I'm an optimist. But it was difficult to deal with. Why couldn't Dad make it? This has a lot to do with why I attended as many of my kids' events and games as I possibly could.

1st Football team photo – Drew is sitting above David and JR. My notes on the back say I was #28 and we won 3 and lost 4.

Back to bicycles. A group of neighbor kids and I created a motocross course, literally around our house. We converted our regular street bikes into motocross bikes—this was before you could just go out and buy them. The best bike to start with was a Schwinn Fastback, preferably a single-speed with a pedal brake, not the five-speed with shifter. Its frame was the strongest and could withstand all the punishment we could dish out. We removed the banana seat and installed a regular seat. We raised the seat height to fit the rider. We adjusted the rake of the handlebar for the best balance. We removed the street tires in front and rear and replaced them with a knobby dirt type of tire. And, finally, we removed the fenders.

By the end of the summer the yard would never be the same. We had a jump from the driveway, down around the tight turn behind the big tree, up the back side with bumps that got worn in, around the front, and into the driveway to get going as fast as you could for the jump. Or you could ride a wheelie and just show off. Around and around we'd go, day after day. One of the kids had a garage and an older brother, and we'd fix up our bikes. We were always making some kind of modification or fix to someone's bike.

Fall was football. I started in organized football at age ten on the local youth team. We were terrible as a team. The one highlight of this era was the opportunity to play on the field at Tiger Stadium prior to one of the Detroit Lions games. I think I was twelve that year. I played quarterback and linebacker. It was such a thrill to run on the field and hear the early bird arrivals and the parents in the stands cheering. We lost that game too, even though we only played for a quarter. I remember hearing my name over the stadium loudspeaker: "Benz pass, incomplete." After we played, our teams went into the dugouts and bullpens to watch the Lions play.

Winter was sledding, shoveling driveways, and ice skating at outdoor yard rinks (there were two very close). It seems like we had more snow than we get now. There were two really good sledding hills we could walk to. One, near Maple and Southfield, we called Suicide Hill. That hill had a fork in it so you could choose which way to go, and it ended at the edge of the Rouge River. Someone always went home wet and cold.

Izzy lived across the street when we lived on Pierce. She was the local tomboy, growing up with five brothers, four older and one younger. Izzy was a constant while I was at Baldwin and Barnum schools. She was always the first pick when playing baseball or any other pickup games when sides were chosen. She could hit a ball farther, throw it harder, and run faster than me and most other boys her age.

Jen, Izzy, and I used to have goofy eating contests. We would try to put as many saltine crackers as we could into our mouths at one time, or see how many peanut butter crackers we could stuff into our mouths at one time and still talk. These contests would always end up with us laughing so hard, and most of the time a mess being made.

As kids, we had a tremendous amount of freedom compared to kids today. Times were different. "See ya later, come home when the streetlights come on," moms would say. As I've said, we would ride our bikes everywhere. Pickup baseball games were common, sometimes with older, sometimes with younger kids. The more kids, the better the game would be. Izzy would go on to play softball at Seaholm High School, in college, and professionally.

The Oakland A's had the coolest uniforms at the time. I took a toy batting helmet that I had, spray-painted it green with a bright yellow brim, and hand-painted the *A*. Are we seeing a pattern here of making things?

Jen and her neighbor girlfriends made up a group called the "Pierce Street Pixies," who would sing and dance to the AM radio in the driveway. They would set up chairs around some kind of stage. Someone would be the announcer and then the show would start. They actually rehearsed. They would announce when the next show was. Everything was so innocent and free.

Maybe this is common to all kids, but it was difficult for me to live in the moment. When I was twelve, I couldn't wait to be thirteen, and on and on and on.

I guess I thought the next age up had it way better because they could do more things. Or is it that the grass is greener on the other side? It would take a few years, but I would learn to live in the moment and that the grass is not greener on the other side.

Early on in our relationship, Dad would take me to D.O. on Saturdays and let me run around and play all over the office. The art department was like my art class in school, any color marker you could ever imagine, in fine point and blunt-tipped. Beautiful papers, different types of glues, balsa wood, and supplies the designers used to make scale models of the displays. Out in the shop I played on four-wheel dollies amid the crates and stacks of wood. And then there was the whole other world of the welding and metal shop. It looked like all the same stuff Gramps had in his shop/garage. I don't recall ever being bored or not wanting to go in with him. As a dad, Doug had started out great

Junior High

I started at Barnum Junior High in the fall of 1971. It was six houses away and across the ball field—didn't take five minutes to walk it. I rode my bike except when snow got in the way. Now with a gang of friends—Drew, Kathy, Izzy—we looked forward to meeting new friends. I have very good memories from this era. Taking drafting class with old Mr. Phillips, who told us he invented the Phillips screwdriver, haha. Using vellum paper, good 2H and 4H pencils, triangles, T-squares, circle and oval templates to draw shapes first, then parts. The drafting lettering style I was taught is still how I write today, just nowhere near as neat.

It was around this time that I thought maybe I could be an architect or an engineer. In shop class with Mr. W., I made a cast aluminum bird, a small aluminum bowl, and a plastic lid on the metal lathe. We made salad bowls for our moms using the wood lathe. After layering alternate styles and colors of wood together, some made chessboards in the same manner. (Here I am making things again.)

I was asked to be in the advanced math program starting in seventh grade. This program accelerated the learning so that by the end of ninth grade the class would be a whole year ahead of most other ninth graders. We would have the same math classmates for all three years. By our ninth grade year, we had developed a camaraderie of sorts. We sang the *Gilligan's Island* and other TV theme songs as a whole class before the bell rang for class to start. So nerdy, but we had fun and were learning.

In English Comp we had to learn how to write out the first verse of "The Star-Spangled Banner," with punctuation. What a pain that was. I never got why; it just didn't make sense to me. I never passed that assignment and avoided English and writing classes ever after. But I got A's and B's in school without much effort.

Whatever was the season was the sport I was playing. Baseball and football were my favorites, but I also played basketball and wrestled while at Barnum. We had a football team for ninth graders. I was one of the captains and still played quarterback and linebacker. One of our coaches that year would later become the police chief.

Drew and I wanted to put numbers on our helmets, you know, like the pros, so we rode our bikes up to the local hardware store. On the way, I hit a bump in the road and went head over heels over the handlebars and, *crash*, the bike fell on top of me. Luckily for me, the hardware store was right across the street from the fire station. Drew threw the bike off of me, and by then the firemen were rushing across the street. I woke up in the ambulance with a concussion and had to sit out a game. This was the first injury that caused me to miss any games so far. That was a hard week, being at home resting while all the teammates were practicing, and having to miss one game. I was back the next week, no numbers on our helmets.

One year during the Barnum years I went peeking for presents during the Christmas season. I was very eager to figure out what I was getting. One afternoon when no one was home, I went looking. I found all the presents, every single one. I was so excited at the time, finding everything. I never got caught, never confessed. On Christmas morning, the hollow feeling started in my tummy. After the first present I opened, I was nearly sick to my stomach, knowing what I was getting. I kept opening and opening and of course knew what each present was before getting the wrapping off. That was the worst Christmas ever, and since then I have never had the itch to look again.

In the summer between seventh and eighth grade, Dad bought a boat. This was right out of the blue. There had been no previous conversations or any mention of boating of any kind. It was a 1969 Trojan Sedan with twin engines and a flying bridge. We spent every weekend that summer out on the boat. We had it moored at a marina on Lake St. Clair next to one of dad's friends' boats. We would go out on Friday after one of my games, spend the night, go for a cruise somewhere on Saturday, and get home by dinnertime on Sunday.

One weekend at the end of summer I got to go with the adults to Put-in-Bay, an island in Lake Erie. I believe Jen was at her summer horse camp that week. We left Friday afternoon, in a parade of three boats. It was a four- to five-hour cruise across Lake St. Clair, down the Detroit River, and across Lake Erie. It was a beautiful summer afternoon, sun and clouds, a light breeze. Dad asked me to follow the lead boat, and I took the helm, up on the flying bridge, as soon as we got away from the marina buoys. What a way to spend the day.

Things got a little interesting when halfway across Lake Erie no land was visible to the naked eye. I wasn't expecting that; I had a very unsettled feeling, tight in the tummy, sweaty palms. But only a minute went by and then land dead ahead was visible. I gave up the helm at the Put-in-Bay buoys. We docked side by side with our travel buddies, and I was set free on an island. I had never seen anything like this before. There were what seemed like hundreds of boats and thousands of adults, and I was the youngest person I saw all weekend. To me it felt like a *Playboy* magazine gone live. Bras and panties hanging from radio antennas. Adult drinking and debauchery beyond my wildest dreams. It was somewhat overwhelming, but I managed. I slept on the flying bridge and rode around in the marina with our dinghy and tiny little gas motor, all wide-eyed and wow!

I had become interested in girls since the crush on Joanne. I dated Sally in eighth grade and learned I was immune to chicken pox, as we had kissed the day before she got sick. Mom had chicken pox so bad as a kid that it straightened her hair, she told me.

I dated Michele in ninth grade. She was a cheerleader. She grew up in a much stricter home than I did and was very religious. She had three sisters and they all shared the upstairs bedroom. We became close. Then, for reasons I didn't understand at the time, I felt I needed to break up. Looking back, I see that there were changes afoot on many fronts. The breakup was difficult for her to understand and I'm pretty sure she looked at me differently after that. But this relationship had taught me that being really close to someone was possible, and I always think fondly of that year.

The elementary school group of friends had grown significantly and was much larger by the time we left junior high.

Here We Go Again

The summer of 1975 brought another round of changes. Sometime when I was in seventh or eighth grade, Mom had found a pair of ladies' panties in Dad's car. They weren't hers. That was the deal-breaker, according to Mom. She had had a hunch Dad was fooling around. I don't remember any arguments or fights, but it seemed to me that Dad wasn't around as much. Mom and Dad officially divorced on January 1, 1973. So Dad was not home during the last half of eighth grade and my ninth grade year.

In the meantime, Mom found another man. Dad used to hang out at a local bar and Mom would sometimes meet him there. She met another man in that bar. During those days, Dad knew him as another regular, Dick. Dick started to spend more time at our house. Jen and I would say "Goodnight, Dick" when he left, and he would chuckle because it reminded him of the ending of the *Smothers Brothers* TV show.

So then, and it did seem sudden to me, Mom had a new plan. She wanted to sell the house in Birmingham and move in with this man and his family. He had just recently gone through a divorce of his own and had custody of his kids. Mary Beth was my age, and Richie was a year or two behind Jen.

All through Barnum I had thought, *I'm getting ready to go to high school at Seaholm.* But Dick lived in the cross-town rival Groves area of town. I didn't like the idea of having to go to Groves High School. Mom did some R&D and discovered that Birmingham had an open enrollment policy. As long as you provided your own transportation, you could go to whichever school you wanted to in the district. Well, that's better, I thought, but still, combining two families? Jen would have to go a different junior high, as Barnum had closed, but she could potentially still go to Seaholm as well.

Mom sold the old house in Birmingham and we moved in with Dick, Mary Beth, and Richie. Our own little Brady Bunch.

Big adjustments—I was thankful for friends during this time. By now I'd spent many nights on Kathy's porch talking with her about life. My life, her life. She was the daughter of a local police officer, and we solved all of ours and the world's problems. We decided to remain as friends so as not to deal with a potential breakup if we became more than friends. She was a grounding force in my life during those crazy Baldwin and Barnum years. Kathy has become a guidance counselor, and I was one of her first clients.

We moved in August of 1975, to a subdivision in the 13 Mile Road and Southfield area on a street called Rock Creek: 30365 Rock Creek. I shared a bedroom with Richie, Jen got her own room, and Mary Beth kept her old room. It was nice, but football practice had started and I was as busy as ever with orientation and learning a new school. School started and we all fell into the daily activities of going to school and work, with family dinners for whoever was home. Mom had done a bunch of redecorating to help make herself comfortable.

It quickly became apparent that Mom's rules for us were much stricter than Dick's were with his kids. As we grew older this would become more problematic for me. Other than that, high school life at home seemed okay. It was much different than we were used to, but we all settled in fairly quickly. I played quarterback and linebacker on the JV team that year, adjusted well to life at Seaholm, and met tons of new friends, the gang getting bigger all the time. One of the new friends was Scott; later he would be my best man. He and I met during football practice and soon became best buds.

I was busy with my life, Jen with hers, and so on. Jen and I would sometimes go to visit Dad (Doug) and his new wife. Yes, he remarried and would go on to have children with Karla. Paul had left the picture following our adoption by Doug, until later.

Mom and Dick got married in a small ceremony on Mom's birthday, March 12, in 1976.

That winter of 1976, Paul came back into our lives. He was in town for a work conference or something and wanted to get together for a visit. Mom approved, and we made it happen. He came to the Rock Creek house and we had a nice visit. Jen was there also. It was apparent then: there was no doubt he was my father. The physical resemblance, stature, way of talking were seen and heard by everyone. I mention that because it had come up previously that in order for Doug to adopt Jen and me, Paul had to surrender his parental rights. He had to sign his name on a legal document for the adoption to happen. There had been some rumors that Paul thought Jen and I were not his children. I heard different versions of why they divorced from both Mom and Paul over the years, but in the end, what happened doesn't matter.

At the end of the visit, Jen and I were invited to visit Paul in his new home in Wisconsin. This was all very confusing to me. Paul, Doug, and Dick, all some sort of dad/father. I just wanted one. Dad. I began to question why Paul would give up his parental rights. I did ask both him and Mom. They both said they thought it was the right thing for Jen and me at that time. Hmmm. I was not convinced.

As we got through winter and spring came around, JV baseball tryout practices started. I made the team, no problem. As we got closer to Easter and spring break, the coach announced that anyone who missed practices during the break would be off the team—practices were mandatory. Uh-oh! Dick had invited me to be a part of his annual fishing trip to northern Wisconsin. He and his college buddy and their sons took an annual trip to fish for walleye. It was a long drive through the Upper Peninsula to a very remote spot for the whole week, staying in a nice house, all boys. Fork in the road, what was I going to do? I had accepted Dick's invitation before the coach's announcement. Baseball meant everything to me. But I decided I would go on the fishing trip and take my chances with the coach. I talked with the coach after practice prior to leaving so he would know I would be gone, and he reminded me what he had said. I explained my circumstances, new stepfamily and all. But the coach held firm, no exceptions.

So I went on the fishing trip. We had a ton of fun, caught some nice walleye, shot guns, cooked big steaks, had big fires, and told stories. One day we got caught on the lake during a thunderstorm. I had just hooked a walleye, but we were

Sunset over Lake Superior May, 1976

making a run for it to an island that had a shelter. The fish was still on the line as we got the two boats to shore and jumped out to run like hell for cover. This was a big storm, the sky turning all yellow-green, big thunder and lightning.

And then it was over. We took stock, everyone was okay, and we decided to go back out on the lake.

That walleye was still on my line when we got to the boat. I reeled it in and put it with the others we had caught. I still can't believe that fish had stayed on the line.

What a fun trip; the five of us now shared the common bond of that trip together. Dick and I seemed to make a connection. On the long drive back home, we stopped in the UP to watch the sunset over Lake Superior. I happened to have my camera and took a shot of that sunset. It was a beautiful moment and the photo captured it very nicely. I still have it framed and on display today.

It wasn't that I thought Dick was going to become my dad, but he was the man that ran the house I lived in. He was married to Mom, and he and I could get along just fine. I thought the trip was worth whatever happened back home with the JV baseball team. I had figured that when we got back I would talk to the coach again and ask for one more shot.

The day after we got back, I was home when Mom thought I should have been at baseball practice. I had not said anything to her about the consequences before we left on the trip. I then explained what had transpired. Mom was very proud of me and very angry at the coach. Dick was livid. They said they would call the principal and the athletic director or the district superintendent and fight to get me back on the team. I said no, that's not what I want, please don't. I knew the consequences of what I had chosen. Not that I thought it was fair, but I already knew that life wasn't fair. I would find a team to play for that summer—there were plenty of non-school-affiliated baseball programs. So why had I done this? Looking back, it's easy to see that I was searching for a dad. I can't explain it, but at the time I wanted to experience what being Dick's stepson was all about.

Life Isn't Fair

Let's go back to "life isn't fair" for a bit. By now I had plenty of examples of how life isn't fair to draw from. Mom's situation wasn't fair; she should have found her soulmate right from the beginning if life was fair. I wouldn't be searching for a dad if life was fair. The current baseball situation would have worked out better for me had life been fair.

One of my earliest memories illustrating this occurred when Mom, Jen, and I were living in the townhouse behind St. Joseph Hospital off Woodward, just north of the Pontiac border. I was seven, it was the summer of '67, and the racial tension in the city was apparent even to me. I got a new bicycle sometime after school was out before we moved in with Gram and Gramps for the rest of the summer. The very first night I decided to put it away off to the side of the townhouse's back door, but not locked or inside. As it turned out, that was not the thing to do. When I went to go for a ride the next morning, it was long gone. Someone had stolen my brand-new bike. The day after (I swear to this day) I saw an older kid riding it in the neighborhood. New paint job, different bike for him. I asked him about it, and he gave me some lie and said he didn't think it had been repainted, even though you could clearly see through the scratches. Life isn't fair. When we got back to the townhouse later in the summer, just before school started, he crashed the bike and hurt himself pretty good. What goes around, comes around. Faith? Yin and yang?

Karma? To me, it's all of those, I just wasn't aware of it yet. But I felt some level of satisfaction from his injuries.

"Life isn't fair, have faith" is one of my most important principles. If you're taking notes, this is one to highlight. I wish life was fair. I think on some level we all do. But it is not. However, life not being fair is the short-term event. Jen got a bigger piece of cake—that wasn't fair. Or maybe something more serious, like being in the World Trade Center during 9/11, that certainly wasn't fair. But to me it's only that one event. I believe in a higher power. And I have tremendous faith that "what goes around, comes around." I'll get a bigger piece of cake next time. That man will go to jail, or hell. This is the long-term view. Full circle, the balance of yin and yang, karma. I have faith that the higher power will balance it all out in the long view. Yes, it's a leap of faith. So is every other religion or way of explaining things that we humans don't yet understand. But this is the leap that I can get behind.

Summers on Rock Creek were when I would spend time with that neighborhood group. There were tons of kids on the block and nearby. The Rock Creek neighborhood consisted of new houses in a new subdivision, not like the old Birmingham house. Still, there were kids everywhere, yes, with bikes. There was an annual summer block party. What I remember most were the legendary four square games we would play, with kids from junior high to those out of high school. It was common for the game to consist of ten people, sometimes even more. We would play till it was too dark to see the ball and the driveway lines. The Ceccato family had the best driveway, right across the street. Four perfect squares. No chips, no cracks, just perfect for four square.

Mom and Dick had started to spend time with the Sediks, a couple of doors down. I took driving lessons with their daughter Joyce, who was just a grade older. We would ride our bikes through the neighborhood to our driver's ed class and then ride back together. Joyce remembers that shortly after Mom, Jen, and I moved in, she and another neighbor girl came knocking at our front door one Saturday. They couldn't get a lawnmower started and needed to meet the new boy. I went and got the lawnmower started and wondered why they needed me for that. That's how Joyce and I met, having no idea what the future held for us.

I started working as a teenager. I enjoyed the financial rewards and the freedom to spend my own money. I worked for Uncle Carl at Carl's Golfland a number of times. I have fond memories of the spring ball pick. Somewhere around late March or early April, with the ground still half frozen, we would pick golf balls out of the ground. The outfit we wore was waterproof winter boots, winter jacket, gloves, and hat. We used an aluminum tube open at both ends; one end had spring-like flanges that would grab the ball when you stabbed the tube into the ground. The tube held about sixteen balls. When you filled up your tube, it would be emptied into a wire basket. We used a three-foot daisy picker to pry the balls loose from the frozen tundra. One by one, we would pry it loose, pick it, empty the tube, fill the basket, haul the basket to the ball washer. Now the range is covered with artificial turf and the balls don't have to be pried free.

During another stint at Carl's, I had just sold my first pair of golf shoes and, unknown to me, Uncle Carl had observed the whole thing. He came over and said that I had done a very fine job of listening to the customer and getting them what they wanted. He then leaned in close to me and said, "Next time, see if they need socks or shoe polish to go with those shoes." He had a great way of patting you on the back and kicking you in the ass at the same time.

I was looking forward to varsity football at the end of summer. We were going to spend a week at a camp, to bond and get in shape before starting two-a-day practices. We worked hard. We played hard too, but clean, with lots of practical jokes perpetrated by the seniors on the juniors. I thought we had a pretty good team, but I felt the coach's system was way too complicated. For example, the offensive line was making calls on which way to block based on what the defense was playing. Sounds good, but certain plays required a particular blocking scheme in order to work, and often the O line would make the wrong call. We started out bad and finished worse at 1–8, way underperforming according to the potential we all thought we had.

Late fall brought a new girl into my life, Cindy. She was a cheerleader. We had met the previous year. I thought she was cute and asked her out. On our first date, to a Lions game at the Pontiac Silverdome, I forgot where I parked my car and we walked around the parking lot for what seemed like forever before we found it. Somehow, I survived that date and we went on to spend most of the rest of high school together.

A group of us had started to talk about a spring break trip to Ft. Lauderdale. Driving down and back, staying in a dive motel near the beach, and hanging out. I'm not sure how I convinced Mom to let me go, but she did. I drove down with three buddies and stayed in a motel called Cascades right on A1A across the street from the beach in Ft. Lauderdale. There were maybe thirty or so others from school. Really, what a crazy time. It felt like we had moved high school south for the week, except with no school. There were both boys and girls, and we had a blast. Four or five rooms for the boys, same for the girls. I remember the girls lying in the sun by the pool, all lined up, in their bikinis. It just so happened that Cindy's family had a condo a mile or so away, so we got to see each other a few times. We walked along the beach. We stayed up all night before Easter Sunday to get a sunrise photo. I still have that photo framed and on display. Bobby and I had an epic rat-tail towel battle all around the hotel grounds. It reminds me now of the sword duel from the *Princess Bride* movie. Somehow, we all made it there and back in one piece—no tickets, no injuries, nobody in jail.

I'm pretty sure that sometime during my junior year, while falling in love with Cindy, I identified my number one life goal and wrote it down in some notebook: get married one time and live happily ever after, just like Gram and Gramps. I had also, by that time, consciously decided to "make the best of it." This would become one of my ways to live life. I'd sure had enough of "it" by then. I had also decided that I wanted a boy and a girl, just like Jen and me. My dream was starting to come together.

Jen and I continued to see Dad (Doug) on a semi-regular basis, once or twice a month. He had moved but was still local. His wife Karla would soon get pregnant and they would raise a family together, and Jen and I visited to stay connected.

Christmas was odd during the Rock Creek years. We'd have Christmas morning with Mom and Dick, hurry over to Doug's for a quick Christmas with him and that family, and then get back home to go have Rose family Christmas at Gram and Gramps's house. It made for a long day.

I learned to slalom waterski the summer between my junior and senior years. One of Cindy's family friends had a cottage on a local lake, with a boat. We spent a lot of time skiing that and the next summer. Skiing taught me that you take care of things much better when you have paid for them with your own money. I was working jobs in between sports and had saved enough to buy my own slalom ski. In 1977, I spent two hundred dollars for a sixty-five-inch Jobe Honeycomb Bob LaPoint Special. Boy, did I take care of that ski, and I got pretty good at waterskiing as well.

The boat we had was terrible for getting up on water skis. It would drag you for what seemed like forever while it got up enough speed so you could get all the way up on top of the water. I got to where I could cut back and forth pretty well. Not nearly as well as Tom, who could do a flip over the wake. Cindy's family had a compound up north on a lake where their whole family would spend all summer. So I skied during the week and spent the weekends up north with Cindy; those were great summers to write home about.

Fall of my senior year brought a new football coach. Chuck Skinner had been hired to replace the old coach. Coach Skinner wanted to change the culture of our program. Seaholm had not had a winning season in quite a while. He, like the other teammates and me, felt we had pretty good talent. We started what we called a "revolt," and each of us players put a piece of athletic tape on the front of our helmet with the word "REVOLT" on it. And we went to work.

Everything was different—the workouts, the pace of practice, the organization. You could feel the team coming together. We did have a "revolt," knocking Kimball out of the state playoffs and beating cross-town rival Groves, highlighting a 6–3 year, the best record in many, many years. We put Seaholm back on the map, and they made the state playoffs for the first time a few years after I graduated. I played defensive back and running back. Not only were my quarterbacking days over, I was just not tall enough or big enough or fast enough to pursue football post high school.

Following football season, I decided to go visit Paul in Wisconsin. I was looking for a dad, becoming aware of Doug's weaknesses and wondering where I fit in this crazy picture of my life. Doug had a new wife and a family on the way, Paul was in Wisconsin, Dick was doing his stepfather thing. All were trying in their own way. It seemed a bit surreal to me, not really knowing what to make of all this, but making the best of it. Paul and I had a nice visit, played racquetball, went to the mouth of the Mississippi River. We had a nice weekend. But somewhere down deep I couldn't see how it was going to work. Back home I came. This was still very confusing to me.

The balance of my senior year was wonderful. Cindy and I continued to date. I visited a couple of colleges and applied. "Swing Out" was a senior class talent and variety show allowing the seniors to say goodbye to the whole school with the students and teachers present. A group of us boys did the traditional boys ballet to "The Nutcracker." We had practiced many times and got all dressed up as girls in tutus. I had a solo.

Cindy and I hung out, going to dances, going to her parents' compound on Hubbard Lake. For senior prom I wore an off-white tux with chocolate brown trim, and I drove Dick's white Corvette. Seventies fashion was terrible, looking back.

We would have weekend parties at someone's house where the parents were out, and we'd drink and laugh and smoke. The drinking laws had changed, and eighteen-year-olds could now legally drink. That law was a mistake that was quickly overturned. A new show called *Saturday Night Live* had started, and at parties we would stop listening to music to watch this crazy new variety/comedy show.

Home life was fairly stable. Jen was now at Seaholm. I would drive us to school in the morning, but not always home after school, depending on our plans. Drew and I would come home to the Rock Creek house to make our lunch—seniors could leave campus.

I had heard back from colleges. No from University of Michigan, where I really wanted to go, because I didn't have the grades or the test scores. Yes from Michigan State, Miami Ohio, and DePauw. I visited all three and decided DePauw was the right choice. I guess I wanted to leave the state, and Scott was going to DePauw. It made as much sense as anything else to me at the time. Looking back, it was not the reason to pick a school. Cindy had decided to go to Syracuse. How was this going to continue? I took the spring off from baseball for the first time ever to spend more time with Cindy. I was hooked, wanted to find a way to maintain our relationship. I knew it was an uphill battle. Her family had a history of East Coast education.

I had a wonderful graduation party, with all the family and friends, and Uncle Marshall flipping burgers to order. All the yearbooks were passed around and signed, some of us acknowledging we wouldn't see each other for a while. It was a great day, capping off a damn good year. Not everyone has the time of their life in high school. I did.

Not Ready for College

The summer between my senior year and my going off to DePauw in Greencastle, Indiana, did not end the way I would have chosen. I worked for Uncle Carl at Carl's Golfland. I was on the greens crew for the little par 3 golf course. Our shift was 6 a.m. to 2 p.m., cutting the greens and fairways. I enjoyed being outside, the pay was good, but the hours were not so special. Getting up at 5 a.m. was tough, and staying out late made it even tougher. Afternoon naps were common. There were lots of grad parties, up-north celebrations, concerts at Pine Knob. It really was a good summer except that the end of summer brought Cindy and me to an end. Cindy had plans to go to Syracuse and I was off to DePauw. I wanted to stay together and find a way, but she did not.

When I got to DePauw, I heard a new song by Dave Mason called "We Just Disagree." It struck a chord in me that I had never felt before. I had such a heartache. I thought maybe my chance for the perfect wife was gone. I was so compelled that I wrote the lyrics out on paper and mailed them to her, one last final appeal. But I also needed some closure to try to move on, to find a way to make to make the best of it. The balance of that year might have been the loneliest one yet for me, and I have often said I partied enough for all four years that year. I just couldn't connect. I couldn't get over Cindy and tried to hide it by partying. I did just well enough in class to stay enrolled. I joined a fraternity and had too much fun and not enough book work. At the end of the year, the dean asked to see me. I had suspected this was coming. He asked me what my plans were for the following year. I told him I thought it was best for both of us if I did not return. He agreed. I went home for the summer to regroup.

Doug had offered me a job with Design Origins. The pay was pretty good even though I had to pay some rent while living at home. I decided it was a good plan, for the summer at least. I knew I needed to stay active with some kind of schooling and decided to take some classes at Oakland Community College—follow my interests a bit and see what transpired. I registered for a class in advertising layout (the art side) and another in photography. I had been interested in photography a couple of different times in my life. I even considered being a professional photographer during this period. It is very satisfying to take a still image and see it come to life in the darkroom. The darkroom has as much if not more responsibility for the finished image as the camera does. There is so much that can be controlled in the darkroom. I had a 35mm Canon SLR and a bunch of accessories, and I understood what the settings were and how everything worked.

Those classes went well, and working with Dad was going well. We seemed to bond a bit, although I could now see his alcohol issues and got to know probably way more than I should have about his personal life.

I took more classes in the spring, photography again, the darkroom side, and a slide presentation class. We had a darkroom at Design Origins—what a tremendous advantage that was. I took a lot of photos and studied a ton of graphic images, advertising, and other forms of marketing. Design Origins was a full-service trade show display company. We had designers, graphic artists, engineers, a wood shop, a metal shop, a sign shop, skilled union carpenters, and sign painters. All my interests were rolled right up in a nice little niche marketing company, and we fabricated everything we designed and engineered. It became apparent that D.O., as we called it, would become my dream.

Another interest I had at the time was to be a sportscaster, or at least to be involved in sports somehow. But not sportswriting, I hated writing. There was no ESPN back then, very few national sportscasters, and I did not want to end up in some remote city in some remote state doing the local sportscast. Even today I find myself making commentary on the sport I'm watching, often saying what the announcers are about to say. A communications major was not regarded very highly. If I was a kid today, I would consider this as a viable career.

I found a program at Ferris State College, which was known for preparing students for jobs and careers. Things were starting to fall into place for me. I was gaining momentum. I moved to Big Rapids, lived in the dorms, and started back at college. During the first term I met an influential professor and changed my major to advertising, the business side. Definitely back on track. It's amazing what being interested and engaged will do to your motivation levels. I worked hard, especially in business, marketing, and advertising classes. I lived off campus the next couple of years, and after three years at Ferris and two summers at D.O., I earned a BS in advertising from Ferris State College.

Creative Problem Solving was the best class I ever took, Ferris or otherwise. It was an elective in my junior year. Problem solving creatively—the title itself caught my interest. Problem solving happens every day. My days of setting up displays were rife with problems to overcome. I could learn how to do it, get good at it, and make life a bit easier. Here's what I learned. Not that I can boil down a college class in one paragraph, but here goes: Creative problem solving is a four-step process. Step 1 is to identify the problem. It's also the most important step. You must think about the problem in a general, nonspecific way, in a way that will help your brain seek the best solution. It's a difficult concept to explain. For example, let's say our problem is that we have run out of toilet paper in the house during the COVID-19 pandemic. For a family of four, no toilet paper is a problem. During the pandemic, most stores were sold out; it was a very hard product to find. It would be easy to identify the problem as just that, where can we go to buy toilet paper? But I would identify the problem as "What can we use to wipe up after using the bathroom?" These are two very different ways of seeing the issue. Don't get stuck on toilet paper, but rather solve the problem, which is how to get clean.

Step 2 is to identify all the possible solutions. The reason to step back and think in a general sense about the problem is that additional solutions will begin to appear that otherwise would not. Do we have any facial tissue in the house for a short-term solution? What about paper towels? We could use wash cloths. Who has a stock of toilet paper, maybe not even for sale? What about the business where you work? With everyone home during the pandemic and businesses closed, no one was working. I'll bet there would be lots of bath tissue in the rest room at the office. And indeed there was. Problem solved.

Step 3 is to identify the best solution. Most of the time, it will appear very easily if you have a good definition of the problem.

Step 4 is to execute the solution. In our example scenario, I headed to the office and picked up eight rolls from the men's room. The TV show *MacGyver* shows creative problem solving in every episode. Mac used only what he had on his person to get out of each episode's squeeze.

Another example I've used over the years to explain creative problem solving happened a bit later in my career at D.O. We had multiple clients at the Frankfurt Motor Show in Germany. The convention center, or fairgrounds as it was called, was huge, thirteen buildings spread over many acres. I needed to visit all of our clients' exhibits multiple times each day, over a fourteen-day period. How best to accomplish getting around the fairgrounds was how I defined the problem. Rent a car? Motorcycle? Hire a private car so as not to deal with parking? Walk? Skateboard? Bike? Motorized bike or scooter? All kinds of ways and solutions came to me. I decided the best solution was a bicycle. I went out and bought a simple single-speed pedal-brake bike and brought it back in the box. We shipped it (in the box) to the convention center inside of one of the crates that was included with the shipment of display materials. When I got there, I put the bike together and rode it around. It worked like a dream, as I could ride right into the buildings and right to the exhibits. I even figured out how to go up and down the escalators on it. After the show, I shipped it back home and still have it today. Although not a fundamental life tenet, creative problem solving is at the root of every problem I solve every day.

Here's the final story I want to share with you about my time at Ferris. During the first semester of senior year, I took a 400-level Advertising Management class. The class was taught by the influential professor I had met my first year. He had become my advisor and I had connected with him more than with any other professor. He had talked many times about a test he took in college where all you had to do was write your name on the test and hand it in. He was always saying to be sure to follow instructions, whether from your clients, your professors, your parents, or your boss—or the directions for how to set up that cantilevered umbrella that just arrived. He pounded it in.

So, mid-terms came around and he handed out our test. On the front page were the written instructions on how to take the test. When he got all the tests passed out, he said we could begin and that we had the balance of class time to complete the test. I heard the front pages being turned over all around me while I took a second to read the instructions. There in plain English, buried in the second paragraph of instructions, I saw this: "If you have not answered any questions, simply write your name in the appropriate space and turn your test in. You get an A." I looked around, and everyone but me had started to answer the test questions. I made eye contact with the professor and he nodded his head up and down as if he understood. I wrote my name in the appropriate space, got up, turned it in, and walked out the door. I'm the only one that aced that test. Ever since, I've been pretty good at following instructions.

Getting Married

I should probably back up a bit and introduce Joyce. Remember, bike riding to driver's ed? She and I had met when we were both fourteen, and we both thought of each other as neighbor friends, never anything more than that. She did ask me to a dance in high school, but I declined, because Cindy was in the picture.

During Christmas break of my first year at Ferris, I was home. Scott and I had gone out to get reacquainted. We decided to go back to the Rock Creek house. Jen and Joyce were there when we got there. So the four of us hung out for a while and talked about what was going on in our lives. Well, one thing led to another. Joyce and I were laughing and joking, we found ourselves wrestling on the floor for some reason I don't remember now, and then we found ourselves kissing. Whoa! Passionately. I wasn't expecting that. Hmmm, stop looking for love and love finds you? I guess I was finally ready for a new relationship. Yeah. Finally, all seemed to be right with my world again.

After break, I had to go back to Ferris. Joyce was living at home and going to Oakland University. We managed a long-distance romance and fell in love. While we dated I was a frequent guest at their family dinners, which were quite different than what I was used to. Mom, Dad, Mark, Joyce, Craig, twins Lisa and Lora, and I made eight. I was used to getting all the fixings I wanted, not used to eight for dinner. There were maybe five on a good night at home. Dishes usually were only passed one time around and that was all there was—you had to make sure you got what you wanted.

The Sediks celebrated Christmas on Christmas Eve with a family dinner, starting with split pea soup. Then there were presents, and then a midnight mass church service. They had been members of the St. Bede parish since they moved to that neighborhood, with Mark and Joyce going to the elementary school.

We continued to date, fell in love, got through our graduations, and married on October 8, 1983, at St. Bede in Southfield, her family's Catholic church. Getting married in the Catholic church meant having to take a class to help us prepare for married life. I recall a meeting with the priest before the wedding. One of the first things he said was, "Since this is a mixed marriage . . ." and I thought, *Mixed? We're of the same race! Oh, he means mixed religious faiths.* I was baptized Methodist, Joyce Catholic, hence we were "mixed." It seemed odd to me and a bit stuffy. But Joyce and I made it through the classes just fine and found it helpful to have discussed some of these things before living together.

We had a wonderful noon wedding, a reception at a local club, and then went back to Joyce's house on Rock Creek for yet another celebration. After that party we spent our wedding night at a local hotel. What a wonderful day. It seemed to have lasted forever.

The next morning, we drove up to Harbor Springs for a week in the woods together. Mom and Dick had rented us a home in a private development near Harbor Springs. After a wonderful week it was time to get back to reality. We had moved into an apartment in Southfield just before the wedding. Joyce was still working for Fisher Wallpaper and Paint; she had started working there part time while in high school. We agree to wait a few years before having children so as to have some time together, but not too long, because we wanted to be young when our kids had kids.

After graduating from Ferris, it was very important to me to get a job on my own, not just go back to D.O. I needed to prove to myself who I was. I went back to Golfland, working in the shoe department for Uncle Carl, while looking for a "real" job, a career. I was a bit disappointed I couldn't get hired on at an ad agency. There were some really good ones in Detroit, but economic times were a bit depressed in the spring of '83 when I graduated. But I did get an offer from a former partner at D.O. to work with photography for slide presentations and setting up events. It wasn't my dream job, but it was in the right arena, and I'd be working for someone I knew. I spent the next couple of years there, two and a half total if I remember right, before Dad called and made me an offer to come work for D.O. It was too good an offer to turn down at the time. And the time felt right for me. I would come to spend the next twenty-five-odd years at D.O. Now I had another goal: I wanted to run and own this company.

I think it's appropriate to talk a bit about faith and religion. I was baptized in the Methodist Church in White Lake, Michigan. Gram and Gramps went to a Methodist church regularly. Mom did not. As a kid, I spent only occasional time in church but was raised with traditional Christian values and mores. I had the opportunity to take a World Religions class while at DePauw. It might have been the best class I took while there. In addition to exploring the traditional Western monotheistic religions, we also looked at the Eastern religions: Daoism, Buddhism, Hinduism, and some others. It seemed to me then that none of these religions could fully explain all the things in the world that we don't understand. I find it difficult to believe in an afterlife. As long as man has been around, no one has been successful in returning to the living world. All the religions do a very good job of providing a means of grounding people, but they also each seem to have weaknesses or some kind of issue I can't wrap my head around. I couldn't find one that I could get behind. When Joyce and I married, she was having trouble with her Catholic upbringing, not being able to come to grips with all their teachings and beliefs. Today, I would consider myself a man of faith. Not in the traditional sense of being religious. But faith in what I have come to believe, in my rules for life, or commandments, if you will. Tenets, guiding principles. This keeps me grounded and helps guide the way through each day. My desire to fully communicate this to my children is at the root of why I'm now writing.

When I was in my thirties, Gramps had a pretty serious stroke and never recovered. Mom asked me if I wanted to go see him before he passed. I said I wasn't sure and asked her a number of questions about his status, then decided to sleep on it. (On a side note, sleeping on something provides a wonderful opportunity for your subconscious mind to help your conscious mind work on a problem.) I decided that I did not want to go see him one last time; he didn't know who *he* was, let alone me. I did not want this new image of Gramps to replace the way I remembered him

I thought it a great honor that my other male cousins and I were asked to be pallbearers. He was the first real loss in my life. I still think of him often and how he would have made or repaired something that I'm working on. I was able to keep his bench vise and some other hand tools from his garage/shop. I treasure them whenever they get used and don't regret my decision not to see him one final time. But I can sure hear his voice: *God dammit, David* . . . Smiles and tears.

Joyce and I lived in apartments for the first couple of years and then moved into a rented house in Birmingham, very close to my old neighborhood. When spring came around in Birmingham, I started missing baseball, being so close to all my old stomping grounds and ball fields. I decided to give back to the sport and coach youth baseball. I found an opportunity quickly and spent the next three springs and summers, before we had kids, working with fifteen- and sixteen-year-old boys in a local rec league. I loved it, Joyce loved it. She learned how to keep score in the book like a pro. I felt like a kid and enjoyed working with the boys. It was great to get back to throwing a ball around and hitting infield practice, and trying to teach those boys the fundamentals. I was surprised at how much I enjoyed the aspect of teaching and thought it would translate nicely to fatherhood. This was my first time teaching, but not my last.

At this point, in the late 1980s, I was working for Dad, married to Joyce, and we had just bought our first house in Lathrup Village, near both of our families. Families were starting to become more important to me. Joyce and I started thinking it was time to try. I now willingly wanted to go to family events on either side. I was spending tons of time with Dad at work, who by now had other children, Doug and Kyle, with Karla. Doug and Kyle were eighteen and twenty-one years younger than me. They didn't feel like brothers. It felt like Karla tolerated me, and yet something was missing with Dad. Our relationship didn't feel like I thought it should. He said he loved me, but it felt different somehow. It seemed like he did no more than he had to from a dad standpoint, yet he pushed hard professionally. To some it may seem like a blessing to have had three different men trying to get you through life, yet I was still craving a dad. I wanted what I thought I would never get and at the same time was becoming more aware of the kind of dad I wanted to be. The first thing was to make sure to attend as many of my kids' events as possible.

As a young adult and now a married man, I started to think about Mom and why she kept getting married. All four of her husbands had their positives and negatives, just like all of us humans. Humans are an imperfect species. I couldn't understand—was she looking for greener grass? I remember Gram telling me in confidence that she also couldn't understand why Bethie, as she referred to Mom, kept looking for greener grass, when what she had looked pretty good to Gram. She also told me that she liked Paul the best, for whatever that was worth. Looking back now, maybe I should have paid more attention to that point.

Christmas with Gram, Gramps, baby Jessica, Mom and me. 1987

Rose Family Christmas

Since I have started talking about families, let me spend some time on a Rose family tradition: Christmas at Gram and Gramps's. Rose Family Christmas. Oh my, what a group, and what a family I'm related to. Joyce was dumbfounded at her inauguration. A good deal of Christmas was always spent at Gram and Gramps's house, with all Mom's brothers and sisters and their families for dinner, "the program," and presents. There was a minimum of twenty-six; I think we maxed out one time with over fifty people, between additional friends and other relatives.

In the basement, tables were set up that Gramps had made from old doors and threaded pipe, with a chair for everyone. Dinner was a combination of potluck and cooking by Gram. Gram had a small kitchen to begin with, and with all the aunts getting their potluck dishes ready, it was difficult to get from the living room to the basement. Once dinner was ready, Gram said grace and we went family by family through the buffet.

After dinner was "the program." The tables would get taken down and moved around, and chairs would be lined up all the way around the room, with room for all to sit and enjoy each other. Food would get stored and dishes done, all in record time, it seemed. All the cousins would race to get their hands on one of Gram's popcorn balls. Most of the time there were enough to go around. They were so good. Then Gram would call everyone together again and start the program by telling us all about her and Gramps's family goings-on for the year. Then each family would get a turn. They could sing a song, tell us what had happened in the past year, do a skit, anything. Gram made sure that everyone present participated. Cousins would get together and sing Christmas songs; yes, we had songbooks. I played "Silent Night" on a toy organ one year. Another time I sang "We Three Kings" with cousins Carl and Mark. The older cousins once did some kind of doctor/patient skit. One year Jen memorized Dr. Seuss's *How the Grinch Stole Christmas.*

This was important to Gram, to spend the day with her family. Gramps would close the program by reciting a poem, the same poem every year. Gramps said he had to memorize this poem in school. You could almost see his mind remember and his face take on a different look. It seemed out of character for him. We all loved his cadence while he recited, big smile on his face. I've learned since that this poem makes people smile. I have now begun reciting it to my family and can't help but smile when I do.

After the program, yay, it was time for presents. Gram and Gramps had a present under the tree for everyone who was there. Most of the time they were handmade. I still have afghans Gram crocheted. I have an M&M dispenser that Gramps made from a mason jar and a block of wood. One year he made hatchets from stainless steel, with deer horn handles, to give to the male cousins. I still have mine. Gramps made his own version of the triangle golf tee game they have at the Cracker Barrel restaurants. He made rocking chairs for his daughters.

Rose Family Christmas went on until Gram couldn't do it anymore, but Jess and Rob got to be included in the last one. Jess read *I Will Love You Forever* on Mom's lap. It wasn't until after Gram and Gramps had passed and we were talking among the cousins that we fully understood the impact Rose Family Christmas had on us all. And we still talk about those programs when we get together.

Below is a reprint of the poem Gramps recited. Read it aloud and feel the smile.

Apple Blossoms
William Wilsey Martin (1833–1913)

Have you seen an apple orchard in the spring?
In the spring?
An English apple orchard in the spring?
When the spreading trees are hoary,
With their wealth of promise-glory,

And the mavis pipes his story
In the spring!

Have you plucked the apple blossoms in the spring?
In the spring?
And caught their subtle odors in the spring?
Pink buds pouting at the light,
Crumpled petals baby-white,
Just to touch them – a delight!
In the spring!

Have you walk'd beneath the blossoms in the spring?
In the spring?
Beneath the apple blossoms in the spring?
When the pink cascades are falling,
And the sliver brooklets brawling,
And the cuckoo bird is calling,
In the spring!

Have you seen a merry bridal in the spring?
In the spring?
In an English apple-county in the spring?
When the bride and maidens wear
Apple blossoms in their hair,
Apple blossoms everywhere
In the spring!

If you have not, then you know not, in the spring,
In the spring!
Half the color, beauty, wonder of the spring.
No sweet sight I can remember
Half so precious, half so tender,
As the apple blossoms render
In the spring!

Oops, Wrong Plane

In my thirties I started doing a lot of traveling professionally, going to show sites and supervising the setup of clients' displays. My worst travel story has its own name: the "Oops, Wrong Plane" story. I was traveling to Toronto on a Friday afternoon for a setup the next day. I was on flight #556 at 5:55 leaving from gate 56, or something similar to that—all fives and sixes. Flight #555 was called, and I boarded and sat in my seat. No issues, no one tried to claim my seat. After we had taken off, the stewardess welcomed us to our flight to Chicago. I chuckled and pressed the call button. The nightmare had begun.

I got to Chicago O'Hare at six-ish on a Friday evening, and now I needed to get to Toronto. I noticed there was a flight leaving for Toronto from the same concourse, and I asked the counter agent. She felt for me but said I had to go to the main counter—all the way back through the concourse, into another line, at the main ticket counter at O'Hare during rush hour. I ended up on that flight I had seen earlier, but I had to pay for the only seat available, first class. Damn, that was an expensive mistake. I did get to Toronto on Friday and the setup went just fine on Saturday. The show opened Sunday, all good. I headed for the airport thinking that my travels home would go better.

The flight left on time in good weather on Sunday around 7:00 p.m. The weather in Detroit was just fine, according to Joyce during our preflight phone call. It was a very short flight from Toronto to Detroit, only forty-five minutes or so. After about thirty minutes, the captain came on the intercom and said we were going to be in a holding pattern for a bit while the weather cleared up in Detroit. What? Weather clearing in Detroit? We circled for over an hour. I was starting to think about how much fuel the plane had left.

We circled for another half hour before the captain made another announcement that we were being diverted to South Bend, Indiana. What? That made no sense to me. What about Cleveland, Grand Rapids, Chicago? We landed in South Bend and were told to wait on the plane. It was an international flight and had to clear customs; no customs in South Bend. Finally, we were told we could leave the plane but had to stay in the terminal and could not take any luggage, only the carry-on stuff we had when we boarded. We found out that a major fog had rolled in from Toronto to Chicago, and South Bend was the best spot to land.

It was now 10:00 on Sunday night, my luggage was on the plane, and we were hanging in the terminal. Nothing was open; this airport didn't have regularly scheduled flights on Sunday nights. By 11:00, there was still no update from the airline, although the counter agent said they were thinking of busing us back to Detroit. I decided enough was enough and I'd take matters into my own hands. I'd find a way home. *Let's creative problem solve this.*

I went to the rental car counter. I heard the agent telling the guy in front of me that he got the last car on the lot. As I was stepping up to the counter, I developed a strategy. I asked the agent at the counter if a car was available to travel to Detroit, because we'd been rerouted, blah, blah, blah. She got it but said, "Sorry, the guy in front of you got the last car we have." I asked her if she had cars held for passengers who were still planning to arrive in the next few hours. She said yes. I said, those people coming in from Chicago or anywhere in the fogged-in area won't be able to get here to pick up their cars. She agreed with me, and I got a car.

I found a couple of people to share expenses, and we got the car and started driving back to Detroit around midnight on Sunday. We got to Metro airport in Detroit around 6:00 a.m. Monday, returned the rental car, and checked the flight board in the baggage area. Ha, our flight had just landed, and luggage would be available at the carousel. I grabbed my luggage and high-tailed it to my car. I'd left it in the long-term lot on the top level—easy to find. I parked in the same area every time. Finally, I made it to my car. I put the key in the ignition and turned. It turned over but wouldn't catch. *Damn, the car won't start. Ahhhhh! Some force doesn't want me to get home.*

At the time, I drove an '86 Buick Skyhawk with a manual transmission. It had been spotty about starting in damp conditions before, but I didn't have any WD-40 to spray in the points. I was on the top floor; I thought maybe I could push-start it using gravity from the down ramp. I pushed it out of the parking spot, around the corner to the edge of the ramp. It started to go over the edge and I hopped in. I pushed in the clutch, put it in first gear, waited for a bit more speed, and popped the clutch. I damn near hit the windshield—the car sputtered, but I couldn't keep it going. Ahhhh! I got out and pushed the car down the aisle, around the corner, to the edge of the next ramp. I got it going this time and away I went. As I was paying, the temperature light came on and the radiator started smoking. Are you kidding me? I pulled over at the gas station at the airport and opened the hood. I went in and bought an expensive gallon of antifreeze. I found a rag, opened the radiator cap, and sure enough, it needed fluid. I dumped in the whole gallon, put the cap on, and hurried to get on the road before something else happened. I finally made it home about 8:00 a.m. on Monday morning. Damn, that was a long weekend.

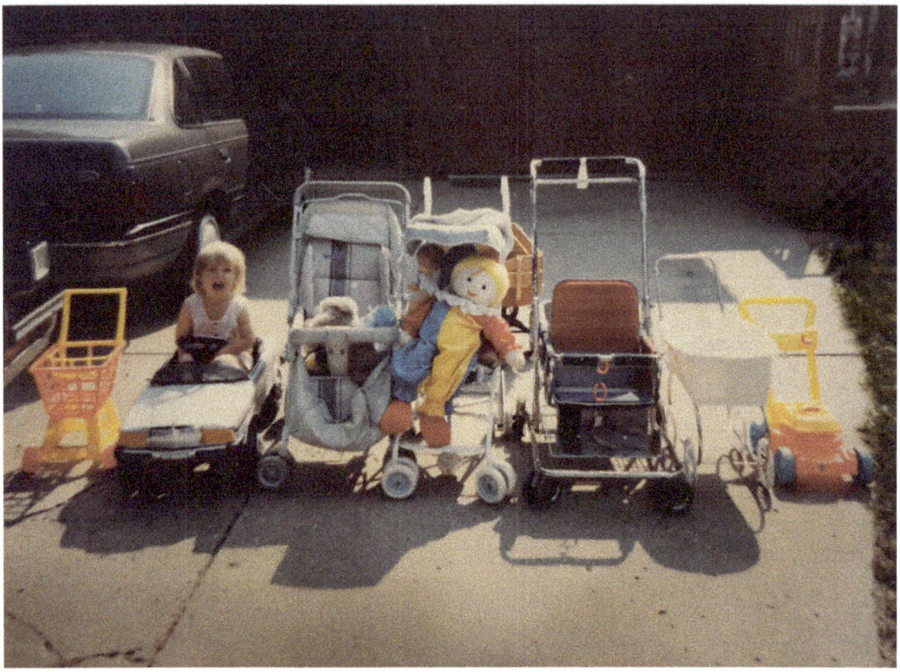

Jessica with all the things all lined up in the driveway. Lathrup Village, 1989

Having a Family

Jessica Lynn was born on October 8, 1987. Robert David was born on March 25, 1989. The feelings I felt on those two days! Words don't do justice. You can't believe you can have that much love for someone so soon after they're born.

It seemed all we had to do was talk about being pregnant and *bam*, Joyce was pregnant. Labor and delivery were a different story; she was in labor for something like thirty hours with Jess. It was better with Rob. Jess was a wonderful baby. Happy most of the time, but a bit stubborn—she wanted to do everything herself. Before she could talk well, she would say "Tata do it." It took Joyce and me a few days to understand that meant "Jessica do it," that Tata was her name for herself.

Joyce had gone back to work when Jessica was three months old, but if she were to go back to work after Rob was born, childcare would cost more than she was making. We weren't sure we could afford to live on just my salary, but it sure did not make any sense for Joyce to go back to work, to pay more than she made for childcare and be away from the kids all day. She wanted to stay home and be a mom. We figured out a way to make ends meet. Rob was not as easy to care for as Jess had been. He was colicky and cried for what seemed like months. One day Dick said, "Give him to me, he won't crack me." Not for a while, but Dick did eventually crack and pass Rob on to another person to hold and comfort. Finally, one night it stopped. I asked Joyce, "Can you hear that?" She said, "What?" The silence. Thank goodness that was over.

Jess and Rob's first day of school 1992

Joyce's parents had moved to Hilton Head Island, South Carolina, shortly after we were married, following their dream. Before the kids were old enough to be in school, Joyce would take them to Hilton Head for a big break. We would all drive down. I would stay a day or two and fly back home to get back to work. Joyce and the kids would spend three or four weeks there before I would fly back and pick them up for the drive home. With all the spring travel I was doing, Joyce needed the extra support. Her parents were wonderful grandparents and the kids have happy memories of being in Hilton Head. I remember going to a local park where Gregg Russell would regularly appear, playing his guitar and singing songs for all the kids. After a year or two, they began to remember the words. We would sing his songs all the way home. "One-eyed, one-horned flying purple people eater . . ." over and over and over again.

I continued to grow professionally and so did our economic situation. Just before Jess started kindergarten, we moved to a bigger house in Troy, with all the space and yard we wanted and still in the Birmingham school district. It was a nice colonial with a very big yard and an in-ground pool. The only reason Joyce agreed to this house with a pool was that you could not get directly to the pool from the house. You had to go outside and through a locked gate. I thought it would be a wonderful house to raise kids in.

We spent our summers between our own backyard and Red Run Golf Club. We made sure both kids were taught how to swim that first summer with the pool. Many a Saturday were spent with me cleaning the pool in the cool of the morning, listening to music. Then the kids, or Joyce and I, or all of us would have friends over and enjoy an afternoon in the pool and later a barbeque dinner.

A few years earlier, our group of friends had started a new Christmas tradition. We called it "The Tree Party." We thank JR and Susan for getting this started. Our families would all get together and go to cut down our family Christmas trees. Then we'd go back to someone's house for a dinner and get-together. Drew, JR, Kathy, and I are now the four alternating hosts. We take a picture of each year's gathering; we have more than thirty of them now, and the "taking of the picture" has become its own little event—trying to corral that many people, kids, and animals into a space large enough. For over thirty years now that tradition has continued. Our children have grown up together, and we all look forward to the next year's Tree Party, as it never fails that we don't get a chance to see each other as often as we would like. It seems that life gets in the way.

Christmas Tree Party photo. 1999

Design Origins

Let's get back to D.O. for a bit. When we left off I had accepted a job working for Dad and D.O. around 1986. I had worked there previously, so I knew some of the current employees, and I knew my way around the departments and the flow of work from one department to another. I started in the sales department, this time working directly for Dad's partner, Hardy. I was running errands, filling out paperwork, learning the different clients, sitting in meetings. Travel started soon after. When traveling, I would be responsible for supervising the setup of one of our clients' displays at a trade show. I worked in convention centers around the country, doing relatively small displays to start with, getting my feet wet.

About three years in, I was given the responsibility to order and coordinate the event services for all of our clients. I had moved from working with relatively small displays to larger and larger exhibits. Freight had to be unloaded, set-up and tear-down labor needed to be hired, electricity and other utilities had to be coordinated. Whatever the client needed while on-site was my responsibility. Shortly after that, I started estimating the event service costs and working on other parts of the sales proposal. It was important to me not to be what I thought might be considered a "typical" owner's son working in the family business. I busted my butt, I didn't want anything be given to me. As new exhibits were being built, I spent time out in the shop to understand how to put them together. I spent time with the designers who were working on new designs so the sales department could anticipate the on-site service costs. I spent time in client meetings, all kinds of different meetings—new clients, existing clients. If it involved one of our clients at a show site, I had my finger in the project.

Maybe four or five years in, I was asked to take the Dale Carnegie course. I'm not sure where the idea originated. I didn't know anything about it, but you know me by now: make the best of it. This was a very beneficial course for me, especially at that time. We learned how to make presentations to a group. We learned about public speaking, problem solving, how to read other people, and the importance of body language. We read three books during the ten- or twelve-week course. *How to Win Friends and Influence People* was my favorite of the three.

At each meeting, each participant would stand and speak to the class about the assignment. I learned a lot and would recommend it to anyone in the early stages of their career. The more you do something, the better you get at it. I believe and understand that from my experience with athletic practices. I'm somewhat gregarious by nature, but this class further nurtured the confidence it takes to make presentations. In my business, making presentations to clients was a weekly occurrence, and you needed to be good, trying to beat the competition. Since that class I have always felt comfortable speaking in public, and I understand the value of being able to make a point, either in a casual conversation among friends or when persuading a client that your solution is the best.

Still Searching

Sometime before both kids were in elementary school, I thought it was important to go and visit Paul. I wanted the kids to have met their biological grandfather, even if I didn't know where he fit in my life. He was now living in the Cleveland area with his wife, Peggy. I was feeling somewhat insecure with Doug, looking to see where I fit.

Joyce was supportive. We loaded up the Skyhawk and headed out for a Saturday/Sunday visit. Overnight, but not too long. It was about a three-and-a-half-hour drive. I had no idea what to expect.

We had a nice visit. It was good to catch up and see where each of us was in life. We continued to stay in touch for a couple of years after that. I even recall a Christmas visit in Troy when he brought the kids presents. Paul wanted to maintain some kind of relationship. I had no idea what that might look like. I had also continued to question why Paul had given up his parental rights so Doug could adopt us. I didn't like the answers given to me by Mom or Paul. Now, since having children, I cannot imagine ever giving up rights to Jess and Rob. Not with a gun held to my head.

I could not find a place for Paul. Sometimes I'm angry about the way things went for me. But that's not productive, and I slip right back into "make the best of it." I am a very pragmatic person and tend not to dwell on the negative. What happened happened, and we can't go back, only forward, making the best of it.

Jen had continued to be in touch and had visited with Paul and encouraged me to reach out. At that point I still didn't know where to put him in a relationship. It was hard for me to see what that looked like. I was working for Doug, still seeing Dick when visiting with Mom, and Paul just didn't seem to fit.

Okay, so I made the best of it, for the short and the long term. You might have heard of the concept of picturing the glass as half full. This signifies a positive outlook. A positive mental attitude, PMA. That's the way I try to look at most everything. Sometimes I do have a bad day, we all do. I try to think about starting the next day fresh. A new day with new opportunities.

I like to tell this story about Rob making the best of it: Rob had surgery on his groin tendon as a seven-year-old, due to a bone disease. The surgeon used a very special method. Each leg was put in a cast from the upper thigh to the ankle. Then a broom handle (really) was placed horizontally between his knees and cast in place to keep his legs spread wide, with his feet about thirty inches apart. The idea was that the groin tendon would grow back longer. He had to wear these casts for six to eight weeks. He could barely get around the first few days, trying to learn to walk all over again without being able to bend his legs. By the fourth week he was break dancing as if his condition were normal, and he could get around at school and at home with ease. He made the best of it. It seems we adults could learn a thing or two from the kids.

I believe it was the next fall, after his surgery, when Rob joined the local Cub Scouts. I had been a Cub Scout. Joyce's family was very committed to the Boy Scouts. Joyce's dad, Harry, had been a troop leader for twenty years. Her brothers, Mark and Craig, had been scouts. I was all-in and agreed to help with the boys. One of my most important tenets is "be prepared." Notetakers, here's another one for you. That's the Cub Scout motto. Being prepared helps you think ahead about what you may need to get ready or get done, whether it's getting the right supplies, studying for a test, leading a big business meeting, whatever.

One thing about being prepared: it's very hard to prepare for something the very first time you do it. That first year in Cub Scouts, when the Pinewood Derby came around, Rob's car didn't finish very well. He was good about doing the majority of the work himself, but he was frustrated that his car was not as fast as the others. The next year was a different story. When Rob told his Uncle Craig, Uncle Mark, and Grampa Harry about his car not doing well, they offered up a whole bunch of suggestions to make his car go faster the next year.

When the next Pinewood Derby came around, he was much better prepared. We spent time planning what to do, going slowly. The big trick in Pinewood Derby is three wheels: offset one of the axles so that one wheel does not touch going down the track. Wheels against the track create friction, and friction slows. So, between the big trick and a bunch of others, Rob won the troop race and got to move on to the next level of competition. This is a good example of both doing your best when you don't know any better and then being prepared and improving—great life skills and not the only skills that scouting teaches.

In the business world, be prepared for your next meeting. Understand what outcome you want to have before the meeting, and prepare accordingly. Think about what you are going to be doing and be prepared, whether for the weather, a meeting, or an uneasy dinner with an unhappy client. You won't give the best presentation if you haven't practiced. Be prepared.

My best work professionally was for the 1991 Society of Automotive Engineers (SAE) show in Detroit. D.O. had won the contract to build the exhibit and create all the content for the General Motors Automotive Components Group. Our concept included a theater for a laser show and individual freestanding exhibits for each of the component divisions. I was put in charge as the project manager. For me, the best part was the laser show. Working with the laser supplier to coordinate effects and timing, writing the script, and going through the approval process were daunting. We hired Patrick Stewart, the new Captain Kirk, for the narration. We recorded Patrick via satellite from a studio in Cleveland while he was in Los Angeles—very high-tech at the time. It took Patrick three takes to nail it. He was so professional; he knew where he could improve it. I certainly was not qualified to give him any direction. I oversaw the music. We created it electronically in the same studio in Cleveland. It all came together and was the star of the show. A photo I took from inside the theater during the laser show made the cover of *Trade Show and Exhibit Manager*. This is the show that would lead D.O. to the international trade show scene.

Tell the Truth

Telling the truth is the foundation under the rest of my life's tenets. Notetakers, this is the most important one. The anchor stone. Everything falls apart like a house of cards in the wind without it. Without truth there is no trust. Without trust, there can be no committed relationship, there is chaos. I always feel better after I've told the truth. The weight of the world is now off my shoulders. We all make mistakes, we're human, but we must man up and accept responsibility. Mom taught me this. She could tell when I was lying and would dig and dig and dig, till she got to the truth. I learned through trial and error that telling the truth always turned out better.

I got pulled over going more than one hundred miles per hour and did not get a ticket—because I told the truth. Seriously. I was coming home after a lobby installation for ArvinMeritor in Columbus, Indiana. I had left after the installation was complete, and we all got back to the hotel at the same time. At the last minute I decided I wanted to play golf at Red Run Golf Club with my buddies on Sunday morning. If I left at midnight, I'd get to the club around 6:30 a.m. Perfect. Have breakfast, play golf, go home and take a nap. It sounded like a great way to end a tough week. So away I went just after midnight.

After an easy drive, I was coming into what I call the "cement canyon," I-696 eastbound just east of Telegraph, where the highway slopes down into a canyon-like feature. Cement road, cement vertical walls, cement bridges—the cement canyon. The sun had just risen, the Kenny Loggins theme song from *Top Gun* came on, and it got me fired up. I was driving a Volvo S-60; it liked to go fast and handled as well as any other car I've ever driven. I turned the volume all the way up, opened the windows, and literally put the pedal to the metal: 80, 90, 100—I don't see anyone anywhere—105. *Wow, this is fast. Woohoo!*

Going by the on-ramp for Greenfield, I spotted a cop in the rearview mirror just turning on his lights. He had seen me. Damn. Foot off the gas, turn indicator, emergency flashers. I pulled off at Woodward before he even got to me. As the officer approached, I had my hands on the wheel, tunes still blaring. "Can you turn that down, sir? License and registration, please." I reached into the glove box for the registration and got my license out of my wallet and handed them over. He then asked, "Where are you going in such a hurry? I clocked you at 108."

I told him the truth. What you just read. He asked about my driving record, and I said, "It's good, no tickets in over five years." He left and went back to check me out. I was sure he was going to write me a big fat speeding ticket. It was pretty clear I was speeding. The officer came back and said, "Thank you for telling me the truth this morning. I hope you have a great round of golf with your buddies, and please, no more Top Gunning." I swear. I sat stunned in disbelief. I said, "Thank you, sir, I hope you have a great day," and pulled away. What a great story I had to tell at breakfast.

Tell the truth. From there everything is possible.

Personal responsibility is very much a part of this for me. Raise your hand when you are wrong, or admit your mistake. It's much easier to move forward. In fact, you can't move forward without it. Minding your P's and Q's is another part. Please and thank you. This is so old school, but so right. I learned this from Gram. You could get damn near anything if you asked properly and said thank you afterwards.

From there it's an easy segue to respect, another guiding tenet. "If you don't have anything nice to say, don't say anything," Gram would admonish. Speak about someone as though they are in the room with you. Be on time. All different ways to demonstrate respect.

I learned a lot from the Japanese about respect. As best as I can tell, it's the foundation of their society. Saving face is about showing respect. In my humble opinion, American society could use a good dose of Japanese respect. While walking down the sidewalk in Tokyo's Ginza shopping district, I saw bicycles unlocked and cars with the windows rolled down, keys in the ignition. There is virtually zero street crime. It seemed unreal, like I was about to be on Candid Camera. That's all about respect for other people's property.

Do you know what time to show up for an 8:00 a.m. meeting in Japan? You better be in your seat, notebook open, pen in hand, ready to rock at 7:55 a.m. (7:45 is okay too). Not being on time shows disrespect for the party you are meeting. Respect is also something that must be earned. You can't disrespect someone or something until you can respect them. Somewhere along the way our society has forgotten that.

Dad's partner, the man who wanted a lit area to read by, was named Hardy Brodersen. I called him Mr. Brodersen until finally, sometime in my late forties, he asked that I call him Hardy. That's respect. At Uncle Carl's funeral recently, I heard many stories of the people that still called him Mr. Rose. That's respect. There was a time when I didn't feel comfortable being called Mr. Benz. (Except when I was in Frankfurt, I was Herr Benz. Somehow it just doesn't come across as formal when it's not your native language.) The son of one of my best bowling buds calls me Mr. Benz. That means something to me. And I knew it meant something to Hardy when I called him Mr. Brodersen. I knew I had earned his respect when I could call him Hardy, another step up the ladder.

Vinnyman

I've been finding ways to laugh since I can remember, but I didn't realize how important laughter is until much later in life. Laughing was probably my first method of diversion from the real world, outside of daydreaming. As a young teenager I listened to comedy albums. Then cassette tapes. Bill Cosby's stories and his ability to tell them are legendary to me. Drew, Scott, JR, and I, as well as others, have learned some of these stories verbatim and will sometimes start in on one just to get a laugh.

During one family vacation, we drove around the whole week with a *Best of Bill Cosby* CD. We never listened to the radio. The kids loved it and now they have their favorites. As I was putting this book together, the story I'm about to tell was one of the first I wrote down in longhand. I wasn't sure where it would fit. Then as I got further along and had come up with my list of tenets to live by, I knew that laughter would make the list. Laugh till it hurts. And then a bit more. It's so healthy. Then your stomach hurts the next day and you get to smile all over again. Did you catch that, notetakers?

Times were good. The four of us—Scott, JR, Drew, and I—felt like we were on top of the world. Scott had just bought a condo in South Florida, sight unseen. This was sometime in the mid to late 1990s. And he had joined a private golf club. (The brokerage business was treating him very well at the time.) Scott and I had met at football practice as incoming high school sophomores. I didn't tell you the whole story earlier. We got into a fight, in full pads, during one of the morning drills. Coach looked at Scott and said, "Benz, you go over to the track that way." Then he looked at me and said, "Hershey, you go to the track that way," pointing in the opposite direction. He had called us by each other's names and ordered us to opposite ends of the track surrounding the field, and we ran, and we ran, and we ran. Coach called us over at the end of the morning session, or we might still be running. We've been best friends ever since.

I've talked about Drew. We became friends during before-the-bell pom-pom sessions on the playground at Baldwin Elementary School. Drew's oldest son, Brandon, has since married my daughter, Jessica. Drew and I met JR during football when we were in sixth grade—See team photo on page 21—and we got reacquainted at Barnum. JR had gone to a different elementary school. JR and Scott had met playing hockey at the outdoor rink in town. Four good friends with a great history of good times, getting-in-trouble times, and times we'll never forget. This is one we will never forget.

The four of us set off for South Florida for a quick vacation. The plan was to scope out the condo, spend a day sprucing it up, cleaning and painting, etc., and spend a couple of days playing golf. Nice long weekend, little bit of painting, lots of golf, laughs with best buddies. Sounded good to me. We had no idea what was in store.

As Scott and I were driving to the airport, I asked him what kind of Vinnyman he'd rented for us four to get around in. He chuckled at the mix-up and said a Chrysler minivan. Little did we know then that that word would become part of our lore. I caught a little grief from the boys during the rental pickup as we got our Vinnyman. Then we were off to find the condo.

By the time we got up the next morning, Scott had finalized his plan of attack. We were going to paint the living room and entryway and give everything else a good scrub. Off to Home Depot for supplies. Paint, brushes, toilet cleaner, bleach, sponges, tape, TP, paper towels, the whole nine yards. And a stop at the party store for the other supplies: liquor, beer, chips, cigs, ice. This was a vacation, you know. And we cleaned, and we painted, like we'd never done before. Certainly our wives had never seen us like this. Scott had said there would be no golf till the condo was done. It's amazing what four motivated men can accomplish in one day.

Scott, Drew, and I were chilling at the end of the day watching SportsCenter and enjoying a beer, some chips, and a couple of puffs in the living room. JR had gone upstairs for a shave and a shower. We all needed a good scrub before we went out for a nice dinner. The condo had two bedrooms upstairs. An open staircase led up to a common landing area, with handrails running up each side of the stairs. From my position on the couch at the time, I had a direct view right up the staircase. The first floor had a kitchen/eating area and a nice pool table in the dining room, which led to a covered porch. The living area was down a step with a fabulous wet bar facing the beautifully landscaped common gardens. There was a couch, a couple of side chairs, a new flat-screen TV—very nice setup. The condo, bought sight unseen, looked pretty good to me.

Over the relative calm of SportsCenter, the leisure of the moment, hanging with the boys, JR comes flying out of the bathroom, bare ass naked, half his face covered in shaving cream. He's screaming bloody murder—about what, we can't yet tell. He grabs the handrails at the top of the stairs with both hands, then swings both feet in front of him, hangs one over each rail, and lands in a cradle, spread-eagled and hanging by hands and feet, nothing touching the ground. Screaming at the top of his lungs. Remember, I'm looking straight up the stairs. I've tried to erase that image from my mind, but I can't—what a sight.

He was screaming with that "this bear is going to kill me" voice, just like Jen did when she saw the snake.

"It's a rat, there's a rat! Came up out of the toilet when I flushed. It's a rat! There's a long-haired sewer rat sitting up on top of the toilet!"

What? Well, that took a minute to register with us three. While Scott was sitting in disbelief, Drew and I ran up the stairs to see what JR had gone nuts about. Sure as shit, sitting on the back edge of the toilet seat like a squirrel waiting for his next handout was a very wet long-haired Florida sewer rat. We exchanged astonished looks and I slammed the door shut. Somehow, we thought to put a towel in the crack under the door to keep him inside the bathroom.

Now what? Being the problem solvers we were, we went searching the condo. For what, we didn't really know. How were we going to get that rat? We opened all the closets and drawers looking for something to take care of it. Scott remembered the small outdoor storage area by the front entrance. Inside we found an old 5-iron and a metal garden rake. Certainly we could kill a rat with those tools. Drew and

I marched up the stairs, 5-iron and rake in hand, men on a mission, when Scott said, "Hang on, you guys are going to go in there swinging like madmen, breaking tile, mirrors, and such, and the rat's gonna run right through your legs and into the condo. No go!" Thank god someone had some common sense. "Let's sit down, have a cocktail, and figure out what to do." Real-world creative problem solving.

By now, JR had calmed down and put on some clothes. He explained what happened while we enjoyed our drinks. I couldn't wait to hear this. All matter-of-fact, JR said that he had taken a dump. Forgetting to flush, he jumped into the shower. He got halfway through shaving when he decided now was the right time to flush. So with half his face shaved, all clean as a whistle, he pushed the handle. The shit went down and up came this rat, swimming his ass off upstream, until he broke the surface and jumped up on the back of the toilet seat. JR had not lost his mind, he had witnessed a remarkable phenomenon—which does happen occasionally, we would come to learn later.

Out came the Yellow Pages; there were no cell phones in those days. Scott found a local guy with rat extermination experience, or so said his ad. JR brought up the Vinnyman thing, and away we went. Vinnyman to the rescue. We had the first Vinnyman coming over to get rid of the rat. He arrived. We asked him if he wanted a beer, and he agreed. He had no bag of stuff, no toolbox, no traps, just a handmade broom handle with a gutter spike duct-taped to one end. Not very high-tech, but it certainly looked capable of killing this rat. Vinnyman went upstairs, and we followed like little boys on an adventure. He was glad we'd stuffed the towel under the door. Before we knew it, he was in the bathroom, door closed, towel back in place.

Vinnyman said the rat was now in the shower. The next sound we heard was the rat screeching. Vinnyman said, "Shit, I bellied him," and we realized we were going to need something to put the rat in. We went hunting and found an empty paint can—perfect. This was starting to come together. The rat was still screeching at the top of its lungs. In went the can, and the screeching started to die down and finally stopped. Vinnyman opened the bathroom door, paint can in one hand, broom handle in the other, and said, "Sorry I bellied him, guys, but he won't give you any more trouble." Scott paid him, and he walked into the night.

So the legend of Vinnyman was born. The new superhero that can fix anything. By then, it was too late to go out for dinner, so we ordered in some pizza and sat down to play euchre. This became the night of our lives as we lived a *Saturday Night Live* episode in real life, all based on this Vinnyman creation that could do anything for anybody. We came up with Vinnyman ads in the Yellow Pages, pretended to leave messages on his voice mail, and created messages Vinnyman would put on his answering machine about the great things he could do. All in made-up cartoon voices, over and over, new skit after new skit. There's no way to remember them all. We were four best buds, sitting around a table playing euchre and laughing for hours on end—so hard my stomach hurt the next day.

We played golf the next couple of days and continued to relive the whole scenario over and over, laughing and laughing. We talk about it to this day. Our wives know the story, our kids know the story. We've each heard each other tell the story, or different parts of it, each of us having our own take on the rat moment. We had art created, T-shirts made up. We had two actual "rat sitting on a toilet" trophies made, custom-molded from pewter, and we played a yearly golf tournament for many years, with the winners keeping the trophies for the year. I have one of those trophies still. I think JR has the other.

Find a way to laugh regularly. Laugh until it hurts, with your friends. Every time I tell the Vinnyman story, or hear it, or sometimes even think about, I laugh. It's wonderful therapy.

Commitment

Gram passed away on February 21, 1999, a few years after Gramps had passed. At church during her funeral, the pastor motioned to where she sat every Sunday for however many years. That space had been left vacant in her honor. I had learned so much from both Gram and Gramps. Now, at 39, I had only memories left. But what great memories they were to me. Uncle Marshall wrote in her eulogy that "Mother was also a gentle woman. She didn't understand violence or cruelty in any form. She would never in her lifetime understand how countries, humans, especially families could harm one another. However, she was the family disciplinarian! Dad usually worked two jobs and wasn't available, so when one of us kids stepped out of the circle, Mother reluctantly doled out the punishment. We all quickly learned that if you started crying before the first blow landed—and maybe ran in a little circle away from the belt—your pride was hurt way more than your rear end. I've always suspected that she cried more about the punishment than we did."

Making a commitment is very fundamental to me. And yes, notetakers, get out the highlighter. I first learned this while playing sports, being part of a team. The JV baseball coach didn't feel I had made the correct commitment to the ball team. I get it. By being away from practices, I hadn't made the same sacrifices the other teammates made during the break and therefore couldn't share in the same level of camaraderie. The other players could have, and some probably would have,

Joyce and me on the Rhine River, Germany. 1999

resented my being allowed back on the team, after it was clear the coach wanted the commitment of the players through the Easter break. I've been one of the players on a team where this type of thing has happened before. When a coach goes back on his word, or allows an exception, team harmony is severely jeopardized.

I stood at the altar at church and made a commitment to Joyce in front of my friends and family. She did also (whew!). Marriage for us is a lifelong commitment. Being committed in marriage means being faithful to your spouse and the marriage. I had plenty of opportunity/temptation to be unfaithful, as well as challenges to my beliefs. Working in the trade show industry, you go where the show is. In my case, that was all over the continent and then all over the world, traveling alone, staying in hotels thousands of miles away. Who's gonna know? I'm gonna know, and I can't, I won't, I'm not going through what Mom went through.

My trick was to try not to put myself in situations where I'd be tempted. I did not hang out in hotel lobby bars, or any bar for that matter. After the workday was done, I would get cleaned up and go out to dinner, making notes for the next day's work. Then straight back to the hotel—I had a busy day coming. I'm not saying it was easy; male anatomy doesn't take no for an answer very well. But it's very rewarding coming home from a trip out of town and, after hugging the kids, feeling the sweet embrace and tender kiss of my wife, welcoming me back home. That's the reward. You feel that in your heart and tell me you don't think your commitment was worth it.

I made sure both Jess and Rob understood commitment. Jess decided at some point in her skating career that she wanted more. More coaching, more ice time, better skates, etc. We asked if she was sure, and she said she was, she was on the verge of making a serious commitment. I don't remember her ever complaining about having to go to practice. The other really cool thing that happens when true commitment is made is found in your heart. You get rewarded for your commitment—an emotional high, such raw happy feelings of accomplishment and joy in completing the commitment.

As Jess made her way from figure skating to team synchronized skating, her time commitment grew and grew. For the last two years of her career, her team made it to the U.S. Nationals. They placed in the top ten nationally. I had never made it to state anything, let alone nationals. She had made the commitment and was rewarded with two trips to nationals and a lifetime of memories.

Rob learned this principle through love of music and the challenge of learning a new piece. He brought a xylophone home from school the day they gave out instruments. This led to snare drums, drum sets, marimbas, and any other percussion instrument out there. Rob played and mastered two pieces in his music career that demanded a tremendous commitment. He had decided on his own to play a Bach violin concerto on the marimba, with four mallets. I didn't know he could play with two. He was able to bring a marimba home, and we kept it in the living room for a semester and a half. He practiced day after day, for six months, six to seven days a week, for one performance. He nailed it.

Then he one-upped it in his senior year. He chose to play "Kitchen Sink" on the snare drum. He also upped his commitment and practiced even more. This piece of music was written especially for the snare drum for a judged performance and was nine pages long. It incorporated every possible aspect: rhythm, syncopation, sound type, loudness level. If it could be done on the snare, it was in this piece. Again, Rob nailed it. I still have the DVD, and it still brings tears to my eyes when I watch it—hell, even while I'm writing this. Rob's reward: two standing ovations and memories for a lifetime.

A corollary to commitment is to "say what you mean, and mean what you say." People who are respectful, people who tell the truth, people who make the best of it, they don't run at the mouth. They listen. They observe. They say what they mean, and then they mean what they say. Think of our president in a cabinet meeting, listening to all the input from everyone around the room and then deciding what to do. He does a lot of listening and observing before he speaks. Or the president of GM in the board room, or a general during battlefield planning. Or the mom at the dinner table trying to settle an argument between the kids. This is especially true in raising children. They learn very early on whether you mean what you say, and they can take over the family if you're not careful.

I think of it as Listen, Listen, (hear) Observe (see, smell, taste, touch), and then you get to Speak. I also like to think about this as using all your senses: sight, hearing, touch, taste, smell. It takes all the senses to observe. Think of Spock telling Captain Kirk that all sensors are activated.

Top Banana

While the kids were growing up, so was my career. The 1990s proved to be very good, professionally speaking. I rose through the ranks from account coordinator to account manager to senior account manager, VP, and finally CEO. I was put in charge of our largest account and grew their business significantly over the decade. D.O. went from being one of two suppliers to this client to being the sole supplier, and then we still grew that business from the inside. We were doing half a million a year with this client when I started, and over $3 million when I left.

Working in the event and trade show industry provided ample opportunity for travel. Mind you, business travel is not vacation travel. When all is said and done, I've had enough travel, especially post 9/11. My first trip internationally was to Tokyo for the Motor Show in 1993. I spent thirty days there, setting up the show, being there during the ten-day show, and then dismantling. During the show's run I had very limited responsibilities; I just had to get the show open and make sure everyone had what they needed.

Each day I would pick an area of Tokyo and go exploring. I saw the Imperial Palace grounds. I found an electronics and hardware market to die for. I discovered chicken yakitori. It's chicken on a skewer, maybe twenty different ways, fried, baked, breaded or not, but always served on a stick. Very good, very quick, found all over town. I had a map and the subway map. The trains ran on time, with English subtitles on the signage. It was a wonderful rail system using all different modes or types of trains, some much older, some very new. But it was a very simple system to navigate. You just had to make sure you got to your destination before the system shut down at midnight! I became the "map guy" when traveling and was always giving directions. I learned a lot about Japanese life just through observation.

I generated the lead that led to D.O.'s winning the big contract for the General Motors Automotive Components Group for the '91 SAE show mentioned earlier. Doug continued to reduce his role over this time period. Hardy was bought out and retired, and Doug became the sole owner of D.O. Shortly thereafter, Doug decided he wanted to move to Gulfport, Mississippi, to partially retire and be closer to his sister, brother, and father. The business had grown to the point where we were bursting at the seams in what was the second building D.O. had occupied. We had thirty thousand square feet of space and thirty-five to fifty employees when things were humming, and we could barely fit.

In late 1998, I came into the office one day and found a banana on my desk. Not a piece of fruit. It was more like a desk ornament, goldish-colored. On the side was engraved "Top Banana." Later that day, Doug asked if I'd gotten the banana. I said yes, but I don't quite get it. He said, "You're now the top banana, I'm going to Mississippi. Keep me in the loop." It felt kind of hollow; no, it felt like more than that, like it wasn't for real. There was no announcement internally, or externally, for that matter. I found out this meant that I was in charge, and Doug was staying on as an employee and maintaining his compensation level. I scratched my head over this. No succession plan, no previous discussions. Just *I'm out, you take over.* Okay, let's make the best of it. I've been dreaming about this—not quite the whole goal of ownership, but certainly running the ship had been a goal of mine.

There were two things I set about early on. From my vantage point as an employee, we needed way more on the computer and IT front. Designers had gone from renderings made with marker or pen-and-ink to digital renderings, which required top-notch hardware and software, and therefore cost top dollar. The next step was to get real with compensation levels for the staff. I had felt underpaid for a while and knew the staff did as well. We started a 401(k) program.

Now we were really bursting at the seams, doing more and more business each year. We started an employee review program. Our client list was growing, sales were growing, but the profit margins were a bit softer as purchasing departments became better educated on our industry. Most of the blame for that went to the General Motors purchasing czar at the time. My most expensive employee was also my least productive and not much help in Mississippi. D.O. joined the Exhibit Designers and Producers Association, and I became an active member and traveled to their national events. We tried to learn from the different business models being used in different parts of the country.

With all the travel and everything going on professionally, how were things at home? Joyce stayed at home with the kids all through their elementary, middle, and high school years. I got very creative in order to attend as many of their events as I could and to be there for family dinners. It was important to me because I'd missed having my dad at my events. Can you imagine playing football all through high school and your dad not making it to even one game? Sometimes I would leave the office early to go to a swim meet and home for dinner with the family, then go back to the office to wrap up my day just before the kids went to bed. It was difficult to find balance with all that was going on; I was so driven to succeed both professionally and at home. I found golf and bowling to be very effective in helping with this—I'll expand on that later.

Just before the end of the decade when the Y2K scare hit, I had decided we needed to move D.O. to a bigger facility. We started looking around in 1998. We found a new business development park nearby and inked a deal to lease a new build-out during 1999, and construction started. We moved in the fall of 2000. We had more than twice as much space, it was organized well, and our designers were involved in the internal design and color scheme. We bought a bunch of new furniture and spent many internal carpenter hours building out the shop, paint, and sign areas to our specifications. And the business continued to grow.

The World Trade Center attacks in 2001 would prove to be very costly in so many ways and drastically changed our industry forever. Events were cancelled, budgets were cut, sales fell, and layoffs were imminent.

The 9/11 attacks had scared people away from flying and traveling in general. But Joyce and I decided we would continue to travel. We had a couple of trips planned and decided not to let the terrorists get in our way. We were going to keep living our lives. One of my high school buddies was getting married, and we wanted to share in their day. We flew to Bobby's wedding in Hawaii in late September, shortly after I had gotten home from Germany. We were the only ones from Michigan who went—even some in Bobby's family did not attend.

Being in Frankfurt, Germany, during these events was another matter. I was at the Frankfurt Motor Show on September 11, 2001, in my client's display area. On a new small flat-screen TV, I watched the airliner fly into the World Trade Center with the same disbelief as you had. This happened the day before I was to leave. I spent five more days in Frankfurt trying to get home. I couldn't get off the European continent. The North American airspace was closed until the fourth day. Talk about lonely. The hotel staff was awesome, incredibly accommodating under the circumstances. The German people were as hospitable to Americans as I could remember. I got home on Sunday, September 16, 2001. The hug and kiss upon that return was impossible to describe. The rush of a zillion feelings all at once. One big celebratory cry.

The next trip we had planned was to visit Doug in Gulfport, Mississippi. We wanted to go in November during the Thanksgiving break. A year or so earlier, he had moved back to where his family was rooted, to retire. Joyce and I had decided we wanted the kids to get to know their grandfather. This visit is one of my best memories of Doug. It was the only time in my life when I really felt he was trying, trying to be a dad, trying to be a grandfather.

We had driven down and stopped in Memphis along the way to visit Graceland and Beale Street and to stay in the Peabody Hotel, which is famous for its duck parades. Jessica surprised us all when she said, "He's still here" as we entered the foyer in Graceland.

We had a great time in Gulfport. We visited New Orleans for a day, had beignets at Café Du Monde, roamed around the French Quarter, had lunch in a bar with great hamburgers—no fries, only baked potatoes. We had a portrait made of Jess and Rob in Jackson Square. We sat by the dock of the bay. There was a bar overlooking Bay St. Louis that was owned by the man who wrote the famous song. We kicked around the little town of Bay St. Louis and bought a metal sculpture of a palm tree. I felt as if finally, maybe, Doug had come around and decided to be a dad. Maybe I had been wrong in my gut before. Joyce and I were all smiles as we left, thankful for a wonderful trip and that the kids made some great memories with their dad's dad.

I've had the opportunity to travel the world. I've been all over North America, Europe, and Japan. Two trips stand out among all the others. Both were with

Rob, Jess, Joyce, Doug and me during our trip to Mississippi while at lunch in the New Orleans French Quarter. 2001

Joyce. The first was our trip to Tokyo. We had made arrangements for the kids to stay with grandparents so she could be gone for a week or so. After the setup was complete for the Tokyo Motor Show, when I had very little day-to-day responsibility, Joyce came over. We stayed in a resort hotel just outside Tokyo near Tokyo Disneyland. It was a short train ride to the convention center in one direction, Tokyo in the other.

We took a day trip to Mt. Fuji on the bullet train. The train ride was fantastic, fast and smooth as well as on time. Once there we decided to take a boat ride around the lake. There was a class of first or second graders on the boat with Joyce and me. We noticed all the kids looking at her and pointing to her blonde hair.

We had quite the tourist experience. One night we went to a nightclub in the Roppongi district, near the Hard Rock Cafe. A local band of four were playing and singing all the old fifties and sixties Motown, Beatles, and Elvis hits, and they were incredible. The music and vocals were right on the money. After one of the sets, I approached them to say thank you. They nodded. They did not speak English.

Me holding up the Great Wall. 1992

They had memorized all the lyrics and didn't understand a lick! We went out for a traditional Japanese formal dinner and toured the Emperor's Palace grounds and other Buddhist temples. We walked to the Ginza shopping district and marveled at the colors in the neon lights. I showed her where I had bought pearls on my previous trip. We had a great time, but finally it was time for me to get back to work, her back to the kids.

The second most memorable trip was to Frankfurt while I was doing the Frankfurt Motor Show. I believe it was our tenth anniversary in 1993. We stayed in the Frankfurt Marriott right across the street from the fairgrounds, very near central downtown and the Hauptbahnhof, the main train station. On one of the early days when I needed to be at the fairgrounds, Joyce took a tour of the Black Forest and the ancient walled city of Baden-Baden.

On another day I took her over to the fairgrounds and showed her our exhibits. We spent a day on the Rhine, taking a trip down the river in a tour boat with a couple of stops along the way. The highlight of the trip was our anniversary dinner at the Zum Storch. Our concierge had recommended it, a very small, quaint, expensive restaurant in the oldest part of town. The setting was very romantic, in a very small old building which had always been a restaurant since it was built in 1704. We were greeted at the door by our host, who knew our names; our concierge had earned his keep! We sat in a small booth in the front of the dimly lit restaurant. We enjoyed a bottle of French champagne with dinner. Once we finished our meal, we asked the waiter to call us a cab. He said the driver was already waiting. It seemed everything had been taken care of by our concierge. We thanked him upon our return and ordered another bottle of champagne to be sent to our room.

Some other highlights from my travels include having lunch at the bottom of the ski hill in Garmisch, Germany, where the 1936 Winter Olympics were held. I drove as fast as I wanted along the Autobahn. I walked the Great Wall of China while in Beijing one year. The air really is terrible there. I stayed in a Japanese hotel in the Jewish district of Mexico City sipping tequila in the English bar on the third floor. The best tableside-made fresh salsa I ever ate was at the Santo Coyote in Guadalajara. I visited Paris for a day. After flying all night from Detroit, I met with clients in the morning and had lunch alone by the Seine River and an afternoon along the Champs-Elysées. I had dinner with clients and a view of the Eiffel Tower before driving by the Louvre and Notre Dame Cathedral on the way back to the hotel. I flew out the next morning. I burned out a clutch in a rental car in Munich, smoked in a café in Amsterdam. I met Cousin Lynn in a bar in Wiesbaden; neither of us knew the other was in Germany at the time.

All the traveling I have done has given me the opportunity to see rich and poor from many countries around the world. To be exposed to customs and ways of life not typical at home. I've experienced having to be frugal as well as living very comfortably. People have asked me over the years how I could be such an optimist, having gone through what I did as a kid. It seems only normal to me. You don't always get what you want, life doesn't play fair. Why spend energy on thoughts/situations/feelings that make you sad? You can always find something positive about anything. There is a silver lining in the dark cloud. A lesson to be learned, if nothing else. When life gives you lemons, make lemonade! Which is another way of saying "make the best of the situation."

A Line in the Sand

Business continued to decline due to the ongoing downturn in the overall economy, and in the spring of 2002 I decided some changes needed to be made. I needed to lower the head count and make some salary cuts. Doug was going to have to participate. He was not going to like it, but it was the only way forward, in my mind. I traveled back to Gulfport in late spring to let him know what my plans were, including his cut. It was taken relatively well. He said I was doing a fine job and to proceed.

So I laid off some people, cut salaries, found a way to balance costs and projected revenue. As much as we reduced costs, sales projections kept declining as the event marketing industry continued to reel from the 9/11 aftershocks. We were going to have to make more severe cuts to survive. I traveled back to Gulfport in the fall of 2002 to present the new plan. He agreed with everything except his cut. I drew a line in the sand: you have to participate, or the plan doesn't work. Things heated up between us. Previously, I had tried to talk about retirement plans and/or buyouts, to no avail. I was getting fed up with the lack of communication between father and son about the future. Doug did not respond well to this at all and told me this time that I was doing a terrible job and to go on home. He planned on coming back to town to rescue his company.

And he did—come back to town, anyway. There were internal meetings, meetings with accountants and attorneys trying to figure out what to do. All kinds of solutions were bandied about. More creative problem solving. Finally, we all agreed on a plan—three of us: Doug, myself, and Sonny. Sonny was our vice president of sales and Doug's brother-in-law. It had been determined that we needed some additional capital to continue operations and get through this. We each agreed to put in $100,000 to provide the capital needed. We agreed on a plan to run the day-to-day business, split between the three of us, with two votes needed to move on big decisions. We seemingly agreed on everything in the spring of 2003.

The day arrived to bring in the money. I brought mine, gathered from my 401(k) and other investments, and Sonny brought his. Doug did not. I don't even remember the explanation. I was dumbfounded. He promised he would have it, not to worry. I was already worried. I had always felt as if he was playing poker in previous meetings and discussions about the company's future, while we were trying to save the company. And now this. Looking back, I never should have made my contribution until his was in as well. No, I should've just walked away. But if I walked away, I walked from my dream to own the company.

Part of the deal was an employment contract with a non-compete clause. I didn't like it, but I was still just trying to keep the company going; I didn't see leaving as a viable option at that time. Not with all the sweat equity and mental anguish I had invested, let alone the $100,000. In what I can only describe as "you can't make this stuff up," the next three or four months were beyond belief from a work standpoint.

I had previously laid off a woman who helped us transition to a digitally based accounting system. The next thing I knew, Doug had hired her back, saying she was instrumental and we couldn't go on without her. He had broken his agreement to vote on big decisions and hired her back without Sonny's or my knowledge. What next? Like I said, you couldn't make up the stuff that happened.

I finally had enough. D. U. N. Done. In a 2003 meeting just before the July 4th break, the three of us found ourselves in a heated discussion about what was going on with the business. I knew by then that I had been right, this wasn't the behavior of a dad toward his son. I truly believe he would not have treated a biological son the same way under a similar set of circumstances. Entering this final meeting, I had prepared a letter of resignation. So had Sonny. We were both willing to walk away from our $100,000 and move on. There was a point in the meeting when I knew the letter was coming out and I was going to have to walk away from the dream of owning the company. I gave Doug my resignation, and Sonny did the same. And we walked out of the meeting and out the door.

The next day we went back to pack up our personal belongings. At this point, Doug wanted to talk to me. He tried to convince me to stay and work it out. As I said, I was done. I used to bleed that company and now things were so bad I had to leave. I'd stayed as long as I could out of loyalty to the staff I'd put together. And I did—I left. Sonny and I believed Doug had violated the agreement we all crafted, and we decided to sue. We wanted the employment contract and the non-compete clause voided. So there I was, suing my father in Macomb County Court. As it turned out, we lost this battle and had to honor the non-compete clause according to the out-of-court settlement.

Doug wanted to talk again after the last court appearance. Again, he tried to find some common ground. At this point I told him what I thought was going to happen: "I will honor the non-compete clause and any other covenants in the settlement. You will fall behind in your line of credit with the bank because you will lose business as a result of this. You will fall out of formula with the credit line, and the bank will take control. You will lose the company and all of its assets. You may have to file for personal bankruptcy. Nobody wins, Dad. But I get to move on with a clear conscience." And that was the last time I ever saw Doug. He died in me that day.

The two-year struggle to keep the company going, fighting with my dad, and things outside of my control, like the overall economy, were hard on me emotionally. I had to let go of a dream, see a goal be unable to be fulfilled. Seemed like it was time to make the best of it again.

So there I was in July 2003, at home, not working, for the first time I could remember. In fact, Jessica was the only person working that summer, having just been hired by Nordstrom in the new Somerset Mall. Joyce was still an at-home mom. Rob was home from high school for the summer. We had saved and had a rainy-day fund for just such a situation. We had saved enough money to maintain our lifestyle and enjoy the summer. A real-life example of being prepared.

And then I got a call, then another. Word was leaking out, and other companies in the industry wanted to hire me. I was being recruited. That was a new feeling. I had anticipated being wanted by others, but you are never sure until it happens. I moved slowly, wanting to appreciate the summer, and not being able to compete with D.O. until January 1, 2004. By the end of summer both Sonny and I had decided to join the same firm. We started in October to learn our way around the company and its systems. We did not make a phone call or do anything else that might have been considered competing with D.O. On New Year's Day at 12:01 a.m. we sent an email announcement of our hiring to our previous clients and contacts. I had written a poem announcing our arrival. I modeled the poem after "'Twas the Night Before Christmas." When business opened the following Monday, the phone started to ring.

The bank took control of D.O. a year or so after I left. Doug did indeed have to file for personal bankruptcy. And the end of D.O. was soon at hand.

Joyce had decided to go back to work. Her daily commitment to the kids was reduced as they were in high school. Joyce liked the new Restoration Hardware store at the mall and decided to see if they needed some part-time help. Her previous experience with Fisher Wallpaper proved helpful, and she was hired.

The Cabin

Have you ever heard the saying "When one door closes, another one opens"? I am here to tell you, I'm a believer. I was not in a financial situation to be able to buy Gram and Gramps's cottage when the family sold it, but ever since then, a goal of mine had been to one day have a cabin on a lake in northern Michigan. With the D.O. door firmly shut, the goal to own a cabin became the other door. I believe it was spring of 2003, at Easter dinner with Mom. Jen and her husband, Dan, and all the kids were there. We talked about Joyce's parents buying a cabin. They had found a little cottage on Lake St. Helen about a two-and-a-half-hour drive away. I talked about always having wanted a cabin on a lake. We had an opportunity or two to visit the lake, which had rekindled my childhood memories from Lily Lake.

Before this Easter dinner, Joyce and I were out on her mom and dad's pontoon one afternoon enjoying the lake. Putzing around, we noticed that all along the north shore there were no cabins, no developments, just pristine forest. I had thought all the lakes in Michigan were ringed with cabins. We had fun daydreaming. We started to look at the individual cabins and houses around that little bay. We would judge whether that was the style or size we preferred, and that we liked that deck or that color. We noticed a little green cabin down the way and decided to get closer for a better look. Yes. Yes. Something like that. A little cabin, nice piece of property situated on a small hill. You could see a one-car garage on the street side and a porch on the lake side, with windows facing the lake. I noticed the fireplace chimney. We figured it had two bedrooms, one bath, a kitchen, and a dining/living area. We floated on the pontoon while we enjoyed a cocktail. We imagined sitting on the hill in a couple of Adirondack chairs watching the sunset over the lake. Then we moved along and never thought much about that moment until now, at Easter dinner. When I mentioned this to the group, everyone was interested. We spent more time discussing goals, cabins, lakes, and other memories and enjoyed the balance of Easter.

Since Joyce's parents had bought a cabin, we found ourselves talking about "what ifs" and what we could afford. We had equity in the Troy house that we could use. We looked around the neighborhood where Joyce's parents' cabin was and figured we could afford something off the lake maybe, but certainly not on the lake. Joyce and I talked with Jen and Dan a couple more times after that Easter dinner. They were interested in a cabin as well. The universe was aligning.

From that initial conversation, things moved very fast. The four of us started actively looking for just the right spot for each of us. Joyce and I went up to visit her parents in late April or early May. We took a golf cart ride around the neighborhood to see what might be for sale and what the prices were. Lo and behold, the small green cabin we saw the previous summer was For Sale by Owner. *Yes, of course we want to see this property!* We planned with the owner to visit later in the day. We really liked what we saw. We had been correct about the bed/bath and room configurations. The inside was finished with knotty pine, so typical of Michigan cabins. There was a nice fireplace and mantel. The view from the hill looking to the lake was just what we had imagined. Oh, and the storage barn across the street was available also. This just seemed perfect in so many ways. It was a golf cart ride away from Joyce's parents. It was priced right if Jen and Dan wanted in as well. We immediately told Jen and Dan and made arrangements for them to visit the following weekend. We refinanced the Troy house to come up with our share. Jen and Dan said they were in and ready. The offer and closing went well, and by the fourth of July, we were equal owners of the little green cabin on Lake St. Helen. It pleased Mom to no end to know we had been able to pull this off.

Moving On

Back to the professional world. As I said, Sonny and I sent out the announcement and the phone started ringing. When it wasn't ringing, I was calling somebody to let them know I was back in the game. I had an opportunity to win some business from ArvinMeritor, the previous D.O. client, in April. By the end of June, the end of the trade show season, we had won the contract to be their sole supplier for the following year, taking the business from D.O.

The next few years would be productive and rewarding. The only distractions were those of everyday life, not all the games and BS that had taken place not that long ago. I did well, and the company did well. Three years later, ArvinMeritor put their trade show business back out for bid and we lost the account. Without ArvinMeritor to keep me busy, I got assigned to various projects and accounts and was expected to be chasing new business as well. Chasing new business was not my strong suit. I could see the beginning of the end. I was let go in December of 2009.

Prior to leaving, I had developed alopecia. I was losing hair in nickel-sized spots all over my head. The doctor said this was the stress-induced version. Great, now I have physiological signs of stress. All those years of stress had built up, and it was being expressed in hair loss.

I found myself out of work again, this time in a very different set of circumstances. The Great Recession was upon us. There were no jobs available. Not that I didn't try, but who wants to hire a 50-year-old former CEO to be a whatever? Unemployment did not begin to cover what I had been making. We had a mortgage and other bills to pay. Yes, we had a rainy-day fund, but this was a bit more serious. It would only take eighteen months of mortgage and other living expenses to eat up everything we had saved. The investment of capital in D.O. was proving to be unwise from a personal financial standpoint.

Jess and Rob were in college at this point, Rob in Kalamazoo and Jess living at home and going to Oakland University. Joyce and I spent a lot of time trying to figure out the best solution. We believed that continuing to make mortgage payments long term wouldn't work. We believed some kind of job for me would appear at some point. We determined the best solution was to sell the house, downsize dramatically, change the balance sheet. We ended up having to make up the difference between the selling price and the mortgage balance, but this still put us ahead and, more importantly, controlled costs moving forward. I was asked a couple of times why we didn't just let the home fall into foreclosure. One word: commitment. It wasn't right, in our set of circumstances, for us. I would not have been able to stomach the fact that we did not honor our commitment to the bank. So we sold. And moved. We rented a two-bedroom townhouse in the Birmingham Rail District. Joyce, Jess, and I, making the best of it.

By the time we moved, I had decided on the path forward. I had offers from a number of companies to be a fully commissioned salesperson. I decided sales was the way forward, but I wasn't connecting to most of these offers. It was just not the right set of circumstances.

Jen's husband Dan had been in the garment decoration business for a number of years, providing screen printing and related services. He had also offered me a sales role. I liked the idea of helping to grow a different family business. I was familiar enough with the industry, having used Impression Center's services previously. I could get motivated to knock on doors or make sales calls for this. As I have said, new business development was not my strong suit. I knew and understood all the different elements involved, but I did not enjoy that aspect. I would much rather grow business from inside an existing client—worming my way in deeper and deeper, leveraging one contact to meet another. That I did enjoy.

We were slowly getting our feet back underneath us again. I got back to work. I joined a local networking group to generate leads. I started making phone calls and following up. Things slowly started to pick up. Orders were coming in. Orders were going out. The sales cycle filled up and the flywheel was moving.

There was an embroidery company renting space in the same building as our company. It was on the brink of failure. I started thinking that embroidery might be another way to continue to grow this business, as well as provide me with some additional income. It could be a way to make more lemonade.

Embroidery is an integral part of garment decorating. There was a whole list of potential customers to offer services to: all the current clients ordering screen printing services. I was not in a position to buy any equipment, but I believed this was a real opportunity. Dan agreed, but having just recently bought a building, he was in no position to buy equipment.

The old single-head embroidery machine was still in the building, and the owner agreed to let me learn how to embroider. I spent the whole summer learning. Near the end of summer, we were convinced this was a good way to go, and the previous company was no longer in business. Dan and I asked Mom if we could borrow some money to buy equipment to open an embroidery business. She agreed. We bought the old single-head embroidery machine and started looking for a used four-head so we could be a bit more production-oriented. We called this new company Impression Center Embroidery, or I.C.E. We set it up as an LLC, each of us equal partners financially. I would be responsible for all embroidery, and Dan had plenty on his plate with the screen printing. It seemed that as soon as we got the new (to us) four-head machine, a really good order just walked in the door. I completed the order and got paid very timely. Now officially in business, we opened a bank account and made a nice deposit. Another lemonade stand coming to life.

Somewhere in the early 2010s I was talking with Craig. Craig was a Seaholm alum, a bit younger than me. Jen knew him in high school. We had gotten reacquainted when we both belonged to Red Run Golf Club. He was asking me about our cabin up north. He wanted to know how we came upon this cottage, the story behind it. I told him the story and remembered to tell him about being in the pontoon on the lake and finding it before it was for sale, when Joyce and I were visualizing being on the hill watching a sunset. He asked me if I had ever heard of the Law of Attraction, or the book *The Secret*. At that point I had not. He went on to explain it and gave me the book to read. I am now a believer.

The cabin visualization part of the story is a perfect example of how this law works. As I practice it, I ask the universe for something out loud and then spend a moment thinking about what I asked for, and then continue to think about the topic. Fairly regularly I will ask the universe about a customer that has not placed an order in some time. Not always, but most of the time the customer I asked about will place an order in the near future. I'll ask about customers who are late paying, and payment will come in. It sounds crazy. I get weird looks when I talk about it. All I know is it works enough for me to continue the practice. It helps to explain why I believe there is a higher power. There is no other good way to explain it. It's very similar to religious prayer. I've read examples of practitioners who claim to have won the lottery. I keep trying, but apparently I don't quite have complete command.

Waterskiing Again

I'd like to share more about the cabin at this point. By the late 2000s we were pretty well settled in; we knew the neighbors, some better than others. The splitting of the indoor and outdoor responsibilities was going very well, by my account. Each family respected the other's wishes on when to be up at the cabin and when not to. Sometimes we all went together for "family weekend," as Brittany called it. It was a lot of people for such a little cabin, but we seemed to manage quite well.

In 2007-ish I was out waterskiing with Craig behind his runabout. We had found an old pair of skis and I thought it would be fun to give it a go. I hadn't skied since high school. It was fun to be back on the water again. After we came in, Scott, the neighbor a couple of doors down, came over and we started to talk about skiing. He was an avid skier, had a real ski boat and wondered if I'd like to come with him in the morning. I agreed and looked forward to trying slalom skiing again.

I borrowed Scott's ski that morning and had a wonderful couple of turns that brought back memories of being seventeen on Pine Lake. That feeling of acceleration after a good turn and racing across the wake. We got into the habit of being up at our cabins on the same weekends and became good friends and ski buddies.

After a while, I got the hang of getting up on one ski and was a better slalom skier than I was in high school. I skied more than a hundred times one year. I skied as early as May 5 and as late as October 10.

Rick, the neighbor in between Scott's place and ours, had grown up on this lake and had talked about skiing many times. We kept asking him to join us. Rick had three young children under seven and was always running around after them.

Finally, after three years of watching us go out and ski, Rick agreed and said he would go out with us in the morning if we were going. Perfect. You needed three in the boat to ski, and before Rick joined us, Joyce or Gail, Scott's wife, would be the spotter. We looked forward to seeing Rick ski.

The next morning at about 7:30, the three of us gathered with our gear at Scott's boat. It was midsummer in northern Michigan, the lake was glass, there was no wind and no other boats on the water that we could see. It was cool and crisp as we left Scott's dock with no idea of what was in store.

Rick asked if he could go first so he could "barefoot," since conditions were so ideal. Scott and I looked at each other with a bit of disbelief. Rick went on to tell us how he was going to get up: "deadman" style. He would lie in the water on his back with his feet pointed toward the boat. He would hold the rope at his waist with both hands. Both feet would wrap around the rope, leaving him to ride on his butt for the three bumps of water the boat makes as it accelerates to speed, about thirty-eight miles per hour or so. Once at speed, he would let his feet down from the rope and then he would be "footin'." I'd never seen a footer from inside the boat at that point and didn't know if I believed him or not. He told Scott that when he said, "hammer time," Scott was to hammer the throttle all the way down. Again, Scott and I looked at each other not knowing what to believe.

Rick was telling us all this as he was trying to put on his wetsuit. The one from before kids, thirty pounds ago. He finally got it all the way on and was trying to zip it up. The zipper was in the front, but it sure didn't look to me like it was gonna make it. He got it up to just over his belly button and then said, "That's enough with a life vest on over the top." We laughed out loud.

We were now in the right spot on the lake, and Rick was ready to jump in and get this going. He jumped in off the swim platform and we took out the slack in the line and got Rick and the boat in position. "Hammer time!" he exclaimed, and away we went. He was right: one bump in the water, two, there's the third, and we were just about up to speed. He was riding on his butt with his feet still over the rope. As we got to speed, he started to uncross his legs and lower his feet into position. Very quickly, he was up, the water spray from his heels flying all over. I'd never seen such a spray. This was crazy. Awesome. Unreal. And I was in the boat watching from seventy-five feet away.

He barefooted from one side of the lake to the other, then dropped back on his butt, let go of the rope, and slid to a stop. Like he'd been doing it for years. You've got to be kidding me. That was incredible, something I'd never seen before. When he got back in the boat, he let out a hoot and a holler the whole lake could hear. Then he said, "I told you I could foot." We never doubted him from then on. Scott and I did ski that morning, but compared to that performance we were underwhelming. But what a wonderful morning ski.

For the next four or five years the three of us would ski just about every other weekend from Memorial Day to Labor Day. Three is the perfect number of skiers to have in the boat. By the time each person has skied once, the first one is ready for anther run. Some mornings we'd be out for a couple of hours by the time we were skied out. Sometimes after we came back in, we would share mimosas on Scott's patio and talk about the morning's runs. We met some other skiers on the lake and now put in a slalom course each year. Although we're not as gung ho as we were just a few years ago, we still go out when we can. It makes us old men feel young again for just a fleeting moment before the stiffness comes knocking.

I tell you that story to remind you how important friends are. Although "Have Good Friends" is not on my list of tenets, maybe it should be. I'm fortunate to have some very good close friends. People need someone to talk to, someone who won't judge, someone you can let your hair down or talk about difficult topics with. Humans are social animals; we need our friends to help us share our experiences, push us to new paths, or remind us to stay on the path we're on. Find them and hold on to them, near and dear to your heart.

Tools for Life

Jessica completed her degree and graduated from Oakland University in June 2010. Joyce and I wanted to give her something extra special as a graduation gift. As we started to creatively problem solve what to do, we began writing down our thoughts. We felt she was in need of some tools to help her through life—both literally and figuratively. We also wanted to pass along some sage parental advice and some cash. We came up with what we thought was a great plan. We bought a toolbox and filled it with common household tools anyone would want in their toolbox. A hammer, screwdrivers, pliers, and so on. Joyce and I brainstormed about what advice to give and how to present it. We started writing down different phrases that have been important to us. Words of wisdom. I don't know how many we came up with, but we needed to cull the list. We decided to write out the twenty best and wrap each one in a fifty-dollar bill, and then put those in the toolbox also. Joyce picked ten and I picked ten. They are listed below in no particular order.

- Must have balance, personally and professionally
- Smile! It shows, even on the phone
- Make conscious decisions; no decision is worse than a bad decision
- Measure twice, cut once

- Don't do more than one thing at a time
- Accept responsibility for your actions
- You only have to convince the reflection in the mirror
- Carpe diem
- Beauty shines from the inside out
- Be the best you can be
- The cream always rises to the top
- If you're not moving forward, then by definition you are going backward
- Avoid debt
- When you take nothing for granted, everything is earned
- Tell the truth – especially to yourself
- Make the best of every situation
- Learn from mistakes, yours and others'
- Fashion fades, style is eternal
- Choose wisely
- Keep your goals in plain sight

As you can imagine, this gift was well received. The whole crowd listened to each saying and watched Jessica's expressions as she showed everyone the whole toolbox. We had a wonderful family day celebrating her achievement on the hill overlooking the lake at the small green cabin.

Reaching this point as a parent gets me thinking about how Joyce and I managed to raise the wonderful kids we have been blessed with. Not that each of them didn't have their own days on the "struggle bus," as Jess calls it, but both Jess and Rob have gotten to the stage where we can see the road ahead for them. And we like what we see. Over the years, Joyce and I would talk about how to raise our children. What will we do if this happens? What kind of punishments will we deploy and at what ages? We covered all sorts of things you might expect, and then there are the ones you don't. I think we have come up with a pretty good short list of what being a good parent looks like. I'm glad to share that with you here. These notes are in no particular order of importance. To me they are all of equal value.

- Play with your young kids at their level, literally on the floor with them, and with what interests them, not you. Cardboard boxes are sometimes the best.

- Speak to your children as adults, as you would want to be spoken to.

- Respect your children's interests and ideas—it's their life, not yours to relive.

- Tell the truth to them; expect them to tell you the truth.

- When giving your kids choices, limit the number of choices. Let them choose between peanut butter and jelly or grilled cheese for lunch, not "What do you want for lunch today?" This allows you to have influence in the choice and yet the child gets to make a decision.

- Have one set of rules for the household. This is somewhat easier in a traditional two-parent family and most difficult when split parenting is involved. But to me, it is critical to the kids' morale.

- Back up your spouse, no matter what. If the topic is that important to you, you will already have discussed it. If not, respect your spouse's decision or choice of discipline.

- Respect your child's privacy, but you can't allow them to use privacy in breach-of-trust situations.

- Have family dinners. It is one of the simplest things to do. Get mom, dad, and kids together for dinner. Yes, it gets harder as the kids get older, but if it's important to you, you will find a day or two each week to make it happen. I think this is fundamental for healthy families. The next step is to give each person an opportunity to talk about whatever they want. One of my favorite lead-ins was to share something I had learned that day and ask everyone to share what they had learned since we were last together.

- Expect your kids to behave the way you behave.

Reflecting

Shortly after I.C.E. had gotten underway, Jen and I lost Mom. On February 25, 2013 she passed away while taking an afternoon nap. It sounds as peaceful as the setting actually was—sitting on a couch in front of a fire one afternoon and nodding off and not waking up. Mom had had a stroke a few years back and was never quite the same, but was still able to maintain herself. Jen and I hosted a beautiful service. Our families spent a lot of the time between her death and the funeral remembering the stories of her life. I was at a place in life to greatly appreciate all she had passed on to me over the course of my life. And grateful that my family had spent significant time with Granny, as we called her then.

Prior to Mom's passing I had started to write down memories from my life. I had no idea where this was going, but one part of me convinced the other part to just start writing. Mom's passing had a significant impact on me. I started to get in touch with emotions and feelings I hadn't paid any attention to before. Mom's passing only intensified the memories. They just came pouring out. I had never felt that feeling before, the pen couldn't write fast enough sometimes. Out of a bunch of those memories of Mom, a poem started to develop. First, I'm writing, and then a poem—who is this guy? It was all part of the grieving process and I couldn't help but let it happen. One night the stars aligned and the poem below found its way out of my brain and flowed out through my hand. Once I completed it, I knew I had come to terms and could move on. I thought it could help Jen get through her grieving, so I printed it on nice stationery and rolled it into an old-fashioned scroll held by a nice little ribbon tied in a knot. (I don't do bows.) It brought tears to her eyes, and more back to mine, and as I read it again, I must just pause a bit and enjoy a memory. Hi, Mom!

Family photo Rob, me, Jess, Joyce, Mom, Jen, Drew, Dan and Brittany 2011

You Are Everywhere

Although you are not really there,
I feel you with me everywhere.
We lost you not that long ago,
I've found a way to let that part go.

The wind came from the north that day,
It was cold and crisp as I walked one May.
I sensed you near, but that can't be.
I could remember, that was the key.

Although you are not really there,
I feel you with me everywhere.
In the warm morning sun, on a cold winter day
In the snow that fell all day today

The leaves on the trees are changing their hue
It won't be long now, for a fire to view
Chocolate chip cookies, right out of the oven.
It's all the wonderful smells that I'm lovin'

Although you are not really there,
I feel you with me everywhere.
I hear your voice when you would explain.
The touch of your kiss when I was in pain.

You laughed so hard they say,
The fifth of six from Zelna May.
I hear it now, that cock-a-doodle-do.
When the room was filled, they could too.

Although you are not really there,
I feel you with me everywhere.

I can't read that without thinking of Mom and remembering something. Perhaps you thought of your mom.

The last of my life tenets is balance. (This one will be on the test, too, so get out your highlighter.) It's important to have balance in life. Not balance in the coordination way, although that can help. But a balance between business life and home life. A balance between being a dad and being a husband. A balance between work and play. A balance between the right and left sides of the brain. The following are the five things I try to do to help with balance:

Work hard, play hard. In that order. Your "play hard" can be anything—a bowling league or a golf league, in my case. It could be poker night, racquetball, bike riding; for some, reading is playing hard. It's whatever activity you enjoy that takes your mind off the "work hard." But you must put your work in. Playing hard without the work is not rewarding at all. The idea is to be so involved with your "play hard" activity that you're not thinking about work, school, or whatever your "work hard" is. Balance.

I have been bowling on a league since just after Jess started kindergarten. First on a league with Dan near where he lived, and later in the Red Run league. For the last twenty of those years I've played with basically the same four guys. It has been satisfying on so many levels. Four men from different backgrounds, at different ages, at different stages of life. We laugh, we joke, and we also talk about serious topics. We have become great friends.

Playing hard allows your mind to be free from working hard. Working hard is stressful; it's called work and not fun for a reason. But humans need a break from working hard, and for me playing hard is what is needed. It frees up the mind from thinking about work. Playing hard is like rest for the work brain. Your brain is thinking about playing, not working. So when you do get back to working your brain is fresh and ready. Work hard, play hard.

Not that long ago, Joyce was diagnosed with breast cancer and went successfully through treatment. During the summer of her treatment, weekly golf was an awesome break for me. I told my partner, Gee, who is also a bowling buddy, that I couldn't have done it without him and the break from helping to take care of Joyce. Those three hours, once a week, seemed heaven-sent to me. Having something to look forward to is very important in getting through the everyday grind of life.

Stop and smell the roses. Literally. Take a minute and enjoy the moment. Anytime, anywhere. As the Nike ad said, just do it. I love to get up early on Saturday mornings when I'm at the lake and sit outside in the cool quiet and listen as the lake "wakes up." I love seeing a sunset, anywhere. Life is a gift; find ways to enjoy it.

Do daily good deeds and random acts of kindness. Open doors. Let someone else take the closer parking spot. Slide a cart to the person behind you at the grocery store. Random acts of kindness make you feel good about life and, more important, will make someone else feel good and maybe help put a smile on someone's face.

Be flexible. Raising a family is not about you as a person, it's about the others in the family and their needs and wants. One year when the kids very young, we got an air hockey table. Rob loved to play. At the time we didn't have dining room furniture. We ended up putting the air hockey table in the dining room for the whole year, until Thanksgiving the following year, when it was our turn to host. Rob still talks about playing air hockey in the dining room.

Make conscious decisions. Burying your head in the sand only makes it worse. Think the issue through, make a decision. By conscious, I mean really thinking through the issue and deciding what action to take. How does this fit with balance? When you make good decisions, it's much easier to find balance. When I make a bad decision, it seems as if bad things start happening all over the place. If you make conscious decisions, you will make better decisions overall, which helps in achieving balance.

One of my favorite quotes (and we quote it all the time while bowling) is from *The Karate Kid* movie. Mr. Miyagi says, "You must have balance, Danielsan."

Drew and I jumping rope in the backyard with the kids. 2007

Personal Growth

I think of personal growth not as a tenet, but as an underlying principle. Something like extra credit. Striving to get better in some fashion each day. Learning from your successes as well as your failures. It's not whether or not you'll fall down—you will. But it's how you handle it after the fall that really matters. That's when true character shines through. It's important to me to continue to learn and grow as a person. I follow what my interests are, without regard to how it will help me. It doesn't matter. If you're interested, see where it takes you. Life is a journey; embrace the ride through life with all its ups and downs, twists and turns. Pursuing your interests will give you satisfaction on many levels and continue to provide for personal growth.

I've followed many interests, or topics, over these sixty years and grown in ways I would have never imagined.

I've studied photography in classes, in books, in person, and in the darkroom back in the analog days.

Even while in the event and trade show industry, I continued to follow the advertising industry through trade magazines. I felt that event and trade show marketing should parallel what was being done in the advertising world—integrated marketing before it was a "thing."

I studied the night skies, bought a small telescope and learned where to find the nebulas, star clusters, and planets. I learned which constellations are in the sky at different times of the year. I would buy science magazines when I traveled, so I had current science material to read. I read every Tom Clancy and John Grisham novel for a period of time. Whether for pleasure, business, or personal growth, I always seem to have something around to read. I love bookstores, I can get lost in them.

I learned how to play chess as a kid. I came across a friend of Rob's who was still playing chess as an adult; yes, he was in the Chess Club. He started talking about all the parallels between chess and life. I got intrigued and started playing online with him, as well as with other people I didn't even know (the wonders of today's technology). The strategy and counterstrategy, playing both offense and defense at the same time, is unique to chess. Chess is an activity you can learn at an early age and play as long as your brain allows. Today you can play with people all over the world from your home, against just about any skill level you want. The digital world does have its advantages.

At one point I had thought about being a marine biologist. Dad and I got certified as scuba divers when I was fifteen through a local dive store. I loved the water, and with the boat it was a natural fit. Although it was not something I pursued long term, it still provided experiences to draw from later in life.

Coaching baseball was another experience in personal growth, mine and the kids I coached. I discovered that I enjoyed teaching, helping others learn what I knew. Now, as I reach into my sixties, I find I like teaching a lot. Mentoring others is a very fulfilling endeavor. I'm currently mentoring a nephew who is working for me. Seeing growth in another person that you are involved with is heartwarming and brings incredible satisfaction. A few years ago, I ran into one of the kids I had coached in baseball. He was now a member of the same golf club as I was. We reminisced about those days, and then he said, "Thank you." He was a dad now and was teaching his son some of the drills we used to run at practice. That's as fine a reward as there is; you can't buy that with money. That's why you give back, that's why you pursue your dreams and interests.

I am a competitive person. I try to win, but I love to compete. How you perform under pressure in sports translates very well into how you perform under pressure in your business career. I am an active bowler, as I've said previously. I have been a league bowler for over twenty-five years. I have had team victories as well as individual victories. I've experienced being "in the zone" athletically, where time seems to slow and your awareness of everything around you is as acute as ever. It's an amazing feeling, but also fleeting. I've also experienced just the opposite. Remember, we are humans, not robots. Thank goodness.

Pursue your interests. You will be amazed at where these take you. As you already know, shortly before my mom passed, I started to write down memories I had of growing up. I did not know where it would lead. The more I wrote, the more I remembered. Mom passed and I wrote some more. Then, when I had let it all out, music called my name. I started down a new path: playing, listening, reading anything about music. In addition to regular piano lessons, I took an online classical music history class, and I read books. I started listening to classical music, went to the symphony. I was fully immersed and engaged in playing the piano and learning about music. I started to hear music differently, hearing vocals I didn't hear before, hearing instruments differently, understanding composition and where the composer might be taking us with this piece. I've often said, you don't know what you don't know. I had no idea music would become such a passion. Now I can't imagine the day when I'm not studying some aspect of the music world. I just finished a book, *This Is Your Brain on Music*, by Daniel Levitin. To paraphrase, he says that when listening to music, you use more disparate parts of the brain than in any other activity, except *playing* music. More different parts of the brain are activated by music than by anything else. That's one of the reasons music is so emotional and moving. The emotional areas in the brain have been activated in addition to most of the others.

Keep Moving Forward

Now, just because I have this group of tenets to live by doesn't mean it's easy for me. I have my moments. As I have said, routine daily life can be a grind. Years of mental stress have taken their toll. And I'm human, too. I've made mistakes. I've been wrong. I don't always have the right answer. I have my weaknesses. Joyce and the kids will tell you I can be a real bear sometimes. But having these tenets helps me get back on my feet and moving forward again.

As I'm writing this, I.C.E. (the little lemonade stand, as I call it) has just celebrated its best sales year yet. I got into this business to provide income to help my family get through the worst recession in our lifetime. This lemonade stand has provided me with way more than I ever imagined. Enough income to live all the life I seek right now. Virtually no more stress, the alopecia has gone away. I'm totally in charge of my time. Here are some additional benefits that have come along for the ride:

I was able to offer Rob a job and be right there at a point in his life when he was figuring out his way forward. Rob had moved back to Michigan after being in New Orleans for a few months. He got a job with a new restaurant and helped them open. Shortly thereafter, they let him go. I.C.E. needed some additional labor, so I offered Rob a job. He learned how to embroider and later showed interest in digitizing, creating the software programs for the embroidery machine. When he had learned as much as he could, we sent him to a weekend crash course to learn from the best. What Rob learned during that time was that he was good at thinking the way a computer program needs to be written. He got good at digitizing and was soon doing all our work in-house. When he realized he wanted to write code for websites, I knew he would be leaving soon. Can't hold that back.

A couple of years after Rob left, my nephew Alex came on board. It's been over five years now, and we continue to learn from each other.

I've had the opportunity to spend one day every other week taking care of my new grandsons.

Another nephew, Calvin, spent a summer with us after his college graduation.

When I was actively taking piano lessons, I scheduled them during the business day. They were that important to me.

Each one of these additional benefits is priceless in its own right. Together, all these benefits out of a little embroidery business I call a lemonade stand . . . I can't find the words to do the feelings justice.

As I was writing this, I reached the age of sixty. And I had a thought about how life would look if expressed in a graph. An up-and-down wave as it moves left to right, kind of like an electronic sine wave or an EKG. Each of us has multiple aspects of who we are. Our professional life, our home life, our moods, our physical condition, our relationships, etc., could all be expressed in the same manner—similar to how biorhythms look when graphed, but with more characteristics on the graph. What occurred to me was that it is very hard to get all aspects of your life on an upward trend at the same time. The converse is also true; not very often will all your aspects be on a downward trend. Many of these aspects we have no control over at all. Which leads me back to making the best of it.

While writing, I have noticed some recurring themes that I hadn't noticed before. Learning euchre from Gram and Gramps, watching them play with their friends. Jess and Rob learned euchre from Joyce and me and watched us play with our friends. Another theme is teaching. Over and over again I'm teaching: euchre, baseball, skiing, life skills, professionally. Since I have become more aware of my ability to teach, I find it easier and easier to teach anyone who's willing to listen. Nieces and nephews are favorite targets, since we have family gatherings so often. Mentoring is teaching. I enjoy it and believe I'm pretty good at it. Learning from someone and passing it along is as old as humanity. Using poignant stories is almost as old.

Up until now, there was never a list. These tenets were not written down; they developed over the course of my life. Seeing them written down is somewhat eye-opening. I think it's a pretty good list. I've been looking at it now for a couple of months and I don't think I've missed anything.

It has been quite an adventure for me, letting all these memories find their way through my hands to the keyboard.

In case you weren't taking notes and now you wish you had, here's the one-page executive summary of the ways I try to live each and every day. They are in order of appearance.

1. Know That Life Isn't Fair

    a. Have faith

2. Make the Best of the Situation

    a. Provides for a positive mental attitude

3. Be Prepared

    a. Be a boy scout

4. Tell the Truth

    a. Foundational

5. Show Respect

    a. Personal responsibility

6. Laugh

    a. Often, hard

7. Honor Your Commitments

8. Say What You Mean, Mean What You Say

9. Find Balance

    a. Work hard, play hard

    b. Stop and smell the roses

    c. Do daily good deeds

    d. Be flexible

    e. Make conscious decisions

Extra credit: Personal growth as an underlying principle.
Pursue your interests. Set goals.
Use creative problem solving.

That's how I try to get through each day. Looking at them in list form, it is easy to see how interconnected each one is to the others. The stories continue as life marches on. What stories in your life have helped shape who you are?

Conclusion

I opened this narrative with the purpose of sharing my life's stories with my children. I wanted to help them understand who I am and what made me who I am. Now I believe there was a greater purpose, hidden right in plain sight.

Over the past ten years or so, Joyce and I have lost our parents as well as other important family members. I've spent long hours thinking about their lives and how they intersected with mine, and what I've learned from them, both positive and negative. The crazy twists and turns that lives take. I'm typically not one to live in the past, but as you lose your parents, all their stories come flooding back. And not only to you, but to other family members, who also share their memories. You almost get to relive those moments. Some come with emotions you didn't expect, and some are so vivid it feels as if you have a movie clip going on in your brain.

While working on this book, I asked my sister, Jen, for some dates and pertinent information to help me keep an accurate timeline. You'd think Jen and I would remember all these stories the same way. But it turns out we don't always have the same recollection of particular moments. Two siblings, who grew up together and went through these major life milestones together, don't always remember it the same way. That's fascinating to me.

After Mom passed, Jen rekindled her relationship with Paul. Several times she encouraged me to reach out to him. As you've previously read, I resisted. But I have come to learn that my version of the truth is not necessarily the real version of the truth.

I stated early in this narrative that happily ever after wasn't going to work for Mom and Paul, but I never really knew why. I've since learned that Mom had been cheating on Paul. And that this had crushed Paul's heart. That was the beginning of the end for them. Back in 1963 it was unheard of for a father to gain custody of his children, but that is what he wanted. How could I not have known this? I was dumbfounded. This turned the whole story around. Not that I thought Mom was perfect, far from it. But it so fundamentally changed the narrative. Knowing that one little tidbit would have affected my ability to cope with having a relationship with my birth father. I wasn't angry. But I was eager to call and talk with Paul.

He is now a healthy eighty-three and living in the Cleveland area. I believe this is the greater purpose for my choosing to walk down this path and chronicle my life: to come full circle with Paul Shoemaker, my father. I spent my whole life searching for a dad. As a kid or young adult, how was I to know which father was more relevant or more important than another? I was anxious to talk with him now. I believed there was a place for him in my life. I was eager for Jess and Rob to see him again. I believed Paul would give anything to meet his great-grandchildren, Harry and George. And Rob and Lauren have just had baby Charlotte.

I called Paul on Father's Day. It had been at least twenty-five years since I had last been in touch. It was weird, yes, but right. It was awkward at first, for both of us. But we spent an hour or so just talking. I could hear the smile in his voice. I'm sure he could hear mine. I hung up the phone grinning from ear to ear, Joyce said. We've since shared texts and more conversations. I'm eager for more. We can't get back any of those years, but we can move forward from here. There is definitely a place for him in my life. We've got so much catching up to do.

I've talked previously about the rewards that come when you pursue your interests or make a commitment to accomplish a goal. This part of my story is another perfect example—finding my dad. I'm convinced the universe wanted me to find Paul again. Jen had been trying for several years. But I plodded down this writing path unaware of what was going on.

All the searching for a dad helped me become the father and grandfather that I am today. I wouldn't be who I am without the struggle and the search. I am grateful my children are who they are and who they are still becoming.

All this writing has taken a toll on my piano time. I find it hard to be working at the piano while writing. I hope you have enjoyed my stories and can take away something to help get you through each day. The piano is calling my name. Who knows what tomorrow's story will be?

And the beat goes on . . .

Just the Facts

David Paul Benz: February 5, 1960 – Sparrow Hospital, East Lansing, Michigan

Wife: Joyce Magdalynn Sedik, September 5, 1959

Married October 8, 1983

Daughter: Jessica Lynn Benz

Son: Robert David Benz

Mother: Beth Lorraine Rose, March 12, 1939, to February 25, 2013

Biological Father: Paul Satterfield Shoemaker Jr., February 26, 1937

Adoptive Father: William Douglas Benz

Stepfather: Richard H. Wiggins

Maternal Grandparents: Leon and Zelna (Van Blarcom) Rose

Paternal Grandparents: Paul Satterfield Shoemaker and Mary Adelaide (Bendure) Shoemaker

Sister: Jenifer Beth Goehmann, March 24, 1962 – San Diego, California

Stepsiblings: Mary Beth Wiggins, Richard (Richie) Wiggins

Half Brothers: Doug Jr. and Kyle from Doug's marriage with Karla

Half Sister: Nancy, Dallas and Mom's child – five years younger than Jen

Timeline of Major Milestones

February 26, 1937: Paul Satterfield Shoemaker Jr. is born

March 12, 1939: Beth Lorraine Rose is born

June 29, 1957: Mom (18) marries Paul

February 5, 1960: I am born

March 24, 1962: Jenifer Beth is born

January 1, 1966: Mom (26) and Paul are divorced

They were married for nine years

May 1, 1967: Mom (28) marries Dallas Merrick

May 1, 1968: Mom (29) and Dallas are divorced

They were married for one year exactly (weird)

December 31, 1968: Mom (29) marries William Douglas Benz (Doug)

January 1, 1973: Mom (33) and Doug are divorced

They were married for four years, almost to the day (interesting dates as well)

March 12, 1975: Mom (36) marries Richard Herbert Wiggins (Dick)

September 1, 1997: Mom (58) and Dick are divorced

They were married for 22 years

October 8, 1983: I marry Joyce Magdalynn Sedik

October 6, 1987: Jessica Lynn is born

March 25, 1989: Robert David is born

January 10, 2008: Joyce's mom passes

September 11, 2011: Doug passes

February 25, 2013: Mom passes

December 10, 2014: Jessica marries Brandon James Wettlaufer

August 6, 2016: Rob and Lauren Emily Eavenson are married

December 10, 2016: Harry Leon Wettlaufer is born

July 17, 2018: George David Wettlaufer is born

July 16, 2019: Joyce's dad passes

July 18, 2020: Charlotte Rose Benz is born

Bibliography

http://mayflowerhistory.com/howland

This Is Your Brain on Music, Daniel Levitin

I Will Love You Forever, Caroline Jayne Church

How to Win Friends and Influence People, Dale Carnegie

CPSIA information can be obtained
at www.ICGtesting.com
Printed in the USA
BVHW091737030221
599193BV00013B/2894

9 780578 781358